Died to *Live*

The Woman Who Died Yet Lived To Tell About it

To Sandra,
I hope this book touches
your heart and lifts
your faith in our
Lord. Be Blessed
Donna
Lee

9/20/05

Died to Live

The Woman Who Died Yet Lived To Tell About it

Donna Lee

Pleasant Word

A Division of WINEPRESS PUBLISHING

Pleasant Word (a division of WinePress Publishing, PO Box 428, Enumclaw, WA 98022) functions only as book publisher. As such, the ultimate design, content, editorial accuracy, and views expressed or implied in this work are those of the author.

Unless otherwise noted, all Scriptures are taken from the Holy Bible, New International Version, Copyright © 1973, 1978, 1984 by the International Bible Society. Used by permission of Zondervan Publishing House. The "NIV" and "New International Version" trademarks are registered in the United States Patent and Trademark Office by International Bible Society.

Scripture references marked KJV are taken from the King James Version of the Bible.

Scripture references marked NASB are taken from the New American Standard Bible, © 1960, 1963, 1968, 1971, 1972, 1973, 1975, 1977 by The Lockman Foundation. Used by permission.

ISBN 1-4141-0454-5
Library of Congress Catalog Card Number: 2005903528

DEDICATION

I joyously dedicate this book to Joni Gibbs for standing by me like a sister and never leaving my side; to JoAnn, Daniel, and Junior for being bold in the Lord and going straight to the throne room of God for my healing; to our oldest son, Jimmy Alan, for stepping up and becoming a man and taking care of his dad and brothers with love; to Chris for being there, helping with the house, and writing poems about his true experience so I would know how he felt deep inside; to my son Josh for helping me with the computer and taking pictures of clouds for the cover of my book (All three of you boys are precious gifts from God. And we love you with all our hearts. I could never express in words how proud your father and I are of all of you .What an awesome gift the Lord gave us); to my soon-to-be daughter-in-law Abby for being there to listen to me, for loving us and our son, and being the daughter we never had; to my husband, the love of my life, for standing by my side and becoming the man I always prayed for; to my special friend Betty Buffington that the Lord put into my life, for helping me with the editing and working with me to get my book done by deadline; and to my family and church family for never doubting that our Lord God would come through.

Your sister in Christ

TABLE OF CONTENTS

PREFACE

A Message from Healing Heart Ministries

In October 1998, we were at my niece's house and I fell to the floor. The only thing I could say as the paramedic arrived was that I felt like I was floating above my body! Not knowing what was wrong, I was sent to the hospital and put in CCU. My heart would speed up then slow down and suddenly, it stopped. I had been healthy my whole life. Between Saturday night and Sunday morning we fought for life. We put on the armor of God and got ready for battle. We put on a healing Scripture tape and we stood firm on the Bible and waited for the Lord to come through.

Sunday morning I went into code blue. They had shocked me twice and were doing manual CPR on me; I was not responding. As the machine flat-lined, I went into the brightest light I'd ever seen, illuminating brighter than looking into the sun. It glistened like gold. I could hear and see the nurses working on me as I floated above my body. Then I felt a magnet pulling me up. Oh, what peace I felt; I knew this was the peace beyond understanding the Bible talked about. I saw angels and even the image of our Lord's hands reaching out for me.

Then I heard my niece frantically scream out, "Donna you have to breathe, now!"

I came back into my body. I was put on total life support. The doctors told my family the grave report: if I woke up, I could be brain dead. They needed to do a heart transplant but I was too unstable. With all the family believing in the Lord, a healing light came down from heaven and the Lord healed me. By his stripes I was healed. I was shocked forty-one times in a twenty-four hour period. However, God was not ready for me to stay with him in heaven. At that time God gave me a brand-new heart! I went from total life support to a living testimony that our God does heal. Doctors said it was medically impossible, but I know what's impossible with man is always possible with our God.

God gave me many visions that I would be praying for thousands of people and they would be saved and healed. Since this time I have been on Christian TV, spoken at many churches and cities across central Texas and Kansas sharing my testimony and praying for the sick, and I've seen many miracles. To God be the glory, great things he has done!

Chapter 1

LIFE AS A CHILD

Growing up, my family traveled from city to city. My father was in the Navy so we moved every two years. When I was twelve we moved to Abilene, Texas. My dad had retired after serving twenty-three years in the military. Texas was the one state we had never been to, so here we were. I enrolled in school and started making many friends. I was invited to go to church with a friend of mine named Shari Turk. I really knew very little about church or about the Lord. I had not been in church since I was a little girl. She told me I would like it and it would be fun, so I agreed to go.

This was a Baptist church and when we walked in, it looked like a mansion. Every word the pastor said spoke directly to me. I had never known anyone that could talk to my heart the way this pastor could. He preached a sermon on salvation. I was very young, but as he spoke I understood every word he said. As he gave the altar call for people to be saved, I felt like running down the aisle as fast as I could. I wanted to be saved and I wanted Jesus in my life, so I went forward. Soon after that I was baptized. As I went down and came back up from the water, I knew I would never be the same.

A few weeks later I met another friend named Joni Lee. She asked me if I would like to visit her church. She was eight years old. We asked her mom and she said yes. I was so excited. We got ready and off we went. This church was different from my church. This was an Assembly of God. As I walked in, I felt something different—warm. The people were coming up to you at the door and hugging you. I know now it was the Holy Spirit and our Lord was present in that church. They prayed out loud and that was different from what I was accustomed to.

This was the beginning of my walk with our Lord Jesus. I didn't understand it but I knew this was something I wanted to learn more about. I often hungered for that feeling that I felt at the Assembly of God church. The love just seemed stronger there and made me want to search the Bible more. Joni and I became best friends. Her mom JoAnn, made me and all the other neighborhood children feel right at home. She was very special. She was always singing. I remember her voice echoing through the rooms of their house. She sounded like an angel. When we would come over, she would greet us with a smile and a hug. The love was more apparent there than it had ever been. The whole family truly had God's love, and they showed it.

When I became saved, I never realized this could be a daily walk. My pastor took me through God's Word, explained to me how I could receive strength, and told me the promises in the Bible were mine. I was so excited. I couldn't wait to get home and read them all. So, I searched God's Word and studied the Scriptures. I prayed that God would teach me about himself and his ways. I wanted to experience what others had talked about. As the years passed, my life turned into an amazing adventure.

I met Jimmy, Joni's uncle. He is the love of my life. I knew the first moment I laid eyes on him, he had to be mine. He didn't smoke or drink. Even at my young age of sixteen, that was very hard to find. He was a Christian man, everything I had ever prayed for. I thanked God for him in my life. At age eighteen we were married. Now Joni is my niece. He would sit in his pew at our Baptist church and pray. I could feel the love of God all over him. Sometimes he would even get goose bumps. Oh, how I wanted the relationship that he had with our Lord Jesus. I knew that I had accepted the Lord, read my Bible, and prayed, but I was still missing something. I knew there was so much more; I just wasn't receiving it. Then the daily walk began. I would get up with the Lord and ask him what he wanted for my day. Finally, I heard these words, *I will guide you with mine eyes and I will never leave you. You will have to be still and know that I am God.* Our Lord's plans will surpass all of our plans and dreams that we have for ourselves. We have a mighty, healing Jesus. He will guide our every waking moment if we let him. He has had our life planned since our creation.

Through our life together, Jimmy and I have three sons. They are the light of our lives. We dedicated all of them to our Lord Jesus.

I had been working at Dairy Queen since I was sixteen, but really wanted to be able to stay home with my boys, so when I got pregnant with Josh I decided to start childcare in my home. I loved it. Now I could help raise my sons at home and care for other children the way I wanted mine cared for. I had four little girls under the age of three. They were so precious. We spent a lot of our days watching Christian TV. We would watch TV everyday day right before nap time. We would all say a prayer and I would lay them down.

After I had been watching the girls a few weeks, I started having headaches. They were not like normal headaches. I would see spots, then a warm tingle would go up my arm to my face; then I couldn't see the phone to call anyone and my tongue would go numb so I couldn't talk. It felt like I had been to the dentist. I waited for a short time and just prayed that my voice would come back or someone would show up. I knew the girls would be getting up soon, and I had to be able to talk and see or I would scare them. Right before they started moving around my eyes focused and I was able to talk normally. My prayer had been answered. Our Lord is never late.

I got on the phone and made a doctor's appointment. I thought I was having a stroke. When I went to the doctor, he did MRI that showed normal. He said it was migraines. I would have a headache for two weeks, a really good day, and then the spots would come again. He gave me medicine to go under my tongue so the pain wouldn't be so intense. This went on for about a year. I prayed a lot and stood on the Word of God knowing that he paid a price for my healing with the stripes on his back. I just kept claiming it.

Then the miracle came that changed my life. I knew when the migraines stopped suddenly and I had been healed. Praise God. Jesus had come through and freed my mind. I thought that was the greatest thing the Lord could ever do for me and frankly, if he had never done anything else, this would have kept me praising him all the days of my life. This gave me a new desire and answered a lot of questions I had in the back of my mind about people really getting healed today. Now I was a true believer. Not only had I seen, I had experienced it for myself. As the years went by, I hungered more and more for the things of God. I ministered to everyone that I came in contact with and told them about our healing Jesus. I had my eyes opened to the deeper things of God, and the more I read the Bible the more the Lord opened his Word to me. That's why they say the Bible is alive.

After all the girls and Josh started school, I stopped my childcare and starting praying the Lord would open the door for me to get a job. I love to talk and share with people, so I went to work at a telemarketing company. I could keep my Bible on the desk so that made me happy.

Jimmy quit going to church. He stopped, and we all quit. We started growing farther and farther apart. One night we were going to Arlington, and our car broke down. We were five miles out in the country and we all had to walk. Suddenly, Jimmy stopped and said, "Look up at the heavens."

I looked up and just saw a moon lit sky.

He hugged me and said, "The Lord is telling me if we get back in church, our lives will straighten out." And the very next Sunday we were back. Through our twenty-one years together Jimmy has quit church one other time. This time when he stopped, the children and I started looking for another church home; one that had a children's program. I prayed the Lord would lead me.

Joni met a man named Billy and soon after dating they got married. Joni and I had kept in touch through the years. They had three children. Our children were all about the same age. We had planned it that way. They were going to Bethel Temple, so we decided to visit. When we walked in the door, I knew this was the place God wanted me. The people met you at the door. I felt such a peace at this church. The boys loved it.

For eight years I prayed for Jimmy to come back to the Lord. I even laid out his clothes every Sunday. I just asked God every day that he would just get up and want to go.

One Sunday the children and I had left for church, and when we came home and he had his church clothes on. He had been to the Baptist church. It didn't really matter what church, I just wanted him in church. I thanked God for the answered prayer. I knew our Lord wanted us together as a family, so I told him we would go with him if he wanted us to. I was already a Sunday school teacher and I loved Bethel Temple, but I loved him more. He told me, "You and the boys stay at Bethel Temple and I'll go to the Baptist church." Every Sunday he would come home and ask me what Pastor Frank had preached on. Time and time again, two preachers from two different denominations on two different sides of town were preaching the same thing. I knew this was not coincidental. Our Lord was working everything out for us. Now we shared, speaking Scriptures and the Bible every Sunday over lunch.

My faith grew and grew. Step-by-step he brought me to where I am at today, totally healed. My heart stopped and raced out of control forty-one times in less than twenty-four hours. They had to shock me every five to fifteen minutes all night long. I went from total life support to a living testimony that God does heal. I saw the bright lights and even floated above my body. I received a message telling me what the Lord wanted for my life and many other visions. I pray that this book will touch your heart as I go through the many healings that I have experienced in my life. Be prepared to have your mind, body, and soul touched by our healing Savior, Jesus Christ. The power of prayer is our greatest defense in the world today.

Thy Word is a lamp unto my feet, and a light unto my path (Ps. 119:105 kjv).

I have learned through the years, all the answers are in the Bible. It's time we, as Christians, start searching for what we need in our everyday life. The Lord Jesus is all we need. It says in his Word he will never leave us or forsake us. We believe doctors with prescriptions we can't read. We need to stand on our Bible that we can read. Through our daily prayer life we will know which way to go. He will guide us with his eyes. He's our creator, supplier, and strength, Alpha and Omega, the beginning and the end.

GOD'S HEALING POWER

It was a warm day in August, 1997. By this time my oldest son Jimmy Alan was sixteen, Chris was ten, and Joshua was eight. Joni and Billy had Daniel who was fourteen, Tiffany was eleven, and Brandon was six. I had a desire to tell people about how the Lord Jesus had touched my life. I met a woman named Armedia Sewell at my job. She knew her Bible and understood the Word of God. Every time I talked to her she would explain to me what the Bible said. It didn't matter what we were talking about or what I was going through, she always had a word for me. I would sit near her and listen to every word she said then look it up to make sure it lined up with the Bible.

Another friend that I had known from Bethel Temple years before started working at our telemarketing company. Her name was Jewel Harnis. She was also very in-tune with the Lord and the Holy Spirit. I was still growing daily.

You never reach the level you need to be at with the Lord. He fills your cup till overflowing then he gives you a bigger cup each day with a hunger to spend more time in the Word. As I sat there praying, I wrote the words to this poem:

You are my supplier, you are my strength,
You know what I need before I need it.
You are my deliverer, you are my joy.
You know what I'm going to ask before I ask it.

You are my sunshine on a cloudy day,
The reason I don't go astray.
You lead me through the day and night
You are my everlasting guiding light.

My legs and my feet,
The reason my heart beats.
You tell me what to do,
I open my heart and you come right through.

When I'm down, you lift me up,
And remind me of your great love.
The loving husband and family you have given me
Means more to me that the deepest sea.

Words can't express the love I feel and the hunger for more of you, Lord. My cup runneth over, yet you give me a bigger cup each day. When I think of the journey of my life so far and all my ups and downs, I see how it fell in place with the guidance of your mighty hand. Even when I was going through the valleys in my life, you always had my outcome in sight. I would look up at the heavens and know you were in control, even when I felt out of control. Lord help me today to always tell people about your mighty love. Let your light shine through me. My prayer is to open people's eyes to what I know, feel, and love about you, Lord. No matter what they are going through, you're the answer for everything. Look to the Lord and all his plans will fall into place. He's had this planned since creation.

I sat there in my seat praising God and waiting for my next call. Jewel was sitting beside me reading her Bible and we were talking about what we felt the Lord was saying to us. There was a lot of sickness at work and we had been praying for everyone. We knew that the Word said by his stripes we were healed and that was for all. We were busy claiming the promises for everyone there.

As we were praying, she prophesied over me and said, "Donna, the Lord is going to use you in a mighty way—far more than your human mind could ever conceive or imagine."

I knew that I had a hunger like never before to tell people about the Lord. We ministered to many people. Seven people had accepted the Lord at our office.

I was reading my Bible one morning before work and writing everything that I thought the Lord was trying to tell me. As I prayed silently, I heard in my spirit, *Donna, millions of people will be saved and healed through your hands.* I sat there in amazement as I wrote down what I had heard.

I told Armedia what the Lord had said and asked her to agree in prayer with me that I would know God's will. I wanted desperately to be used for God's glory. My only desire was to let people see Jesus' light shine through me, but I had to learn much more.

I went home that night and couldn't wait to see my husband to tell him. I didn't know how this goal would come to pass, but I knew somehow it would.

Jimmy and I had been married since I was eighteen, and we shared everything. When Jimmy got home, I met him at the door and told him what I felt the Lord was telling me. He said, "Donna, you know the Lord always has a plan and his plans will always come to pass in his timing. Just make sure you stay focused on the Lord, and all others things will fall into place." Both Jimmy and I had grown so much in the Lord.

Joni and I were so close, I knew what she was thinking before she could even tell me. Joni and Billy had been blessed with a wonderful rock house in the country that had ten acres of land with it. This house was a "dream come true." We liked to go to their house on Saturdays and cook out. We loved it as much as they did.

On Saturday October 17, 1998, I had gone to work that morning like I normally did. As I was reading my Bible, I started feeling like I was floating above my body. I honestly thought the Lord was showing me a small taste of his glory as I studied his Word. That morning the calls were coming in slowly, so I went home. This was Saturday and I needed to call Joni. Jimmy, Chris, Josh, and I started for the country. Our oldest son Jimmy Alan had gone to the homecoming dance at Abilene High School.

This was a wonderful family day. I never dreamed that I might end up in CCU fighting for my life. I had always been in good shape, and I had never had any health problems. This day changed my life forever

Chapter 3

A WARM FALL DAY

Joni was washing dishes; I was drying and putting them up. We could hear the men in the living room laughing and having a good time. We were also singing. Our wonderful weekend was about to change forever.

As I reached up to put a glass in the cabinet, down I went. Joni thought I had tripped and was laughing, but my body was shaking profusely. She laughed as she lifted my head to see if I was OK. Fear filled the room when she noticed that my eyes were rolled back in my head. She screamed at the top of her lungs, "Billy, Jimmy, get in here!" By the tone of her voice they knew something was terribly wrong. We had seen many rattlesnakes on their land, so the guys thought maybe one had come into the house. As they hurried into the kitchen, both of them saw me on the floor. Joni was shaking me as hard as she could, trying to wake me.

I remember opening my eyes and asking her, "Where am I?"

She answered by calling my name, "Donna, you don't know where you are?"

I was very distraught for a moment, and then I proceeded to ask her what had happened. Sitting up and seeing the fear on everyone's face, I knew something must be terribly wrong.

"I don't know what happened," Joni said. "We were doing dishes and when you reached toward the cabinet, down you went." I sat there for the longest time just talking to my family. I wanted them to know that I was OK. All the children were in the kitchen by my side. They were crying and really upset. My main concern was that my family knew I was going to be OK. Finally, as I felt rested, I told them I was fine; "Help me up." As they reached to help me up, down I went again. My body went completely limp. My eyes rolled back in my head and I started shaking. My niece, Joni held me and shook me until I woke up. Then they called 911.

I had never seen so much fear on everyone's face as I did that night. I argued with my family that I didn't need to go to the hospital; however, I felt something must be terribly wrong. I kept telling Joni that I felt like I was floating above my body. She screamed, "Hang in there. It can't be too much longer." We were eighteen miles in the country. Although it seemed like it took forever for the ambulance to arrive, really it was only a few minutes. Before we knew it, the house was filled with not only paramedics, but also the sheriff and firemen of Eula. Even neighbors were there. Everyone wanted to help.

The fireman arrived first and talked to me about what had happened. They took my vital signs which were normal. When the ambulance drove up, they all came into the house. As I sat there, they began asking me questions like, "Do you know who you are?"

I just smiled; I thought that was a silly question. Of course I knew who I was. By that time I was feeling much better. I really didn't want to go to the hospital, but my family gave me no choice. They loved me with all their hearts, and they knew there had to be a reason for this happening. So I agreed to go.

They put me on the stretcher and into the ambulance. As we drove off, my family followed closely behind. The paramedics kept me talking. He asked me, "How long have you been married?"

"I've been married twenty years" I replied.

"How many children do you have?"

"I have three sons. They are seventeen, eleven, and nine."

Then he asked me, "How long have you known Joni?"

"We have been best friends since I was twelve years old. At eighteen I married into the family. We have always been very close."

He kept me talking the whole time. I could hear him responding to the hospital with all my vital signs. I had never been sick nor in an ambulance before. In a moment, he started to start an IV. I remember asking him if he could hit the vein while going down the bumpy roads.

He just laughed. He told me, "We are trained to be accurate." I remember praying that he was right. I could imagine that needle going straight through my arm. In the hospital when my children were born, the nurses always had a hard time finding my veins even though at that time we weren't going ninety miles an hour on a bumpy, dirt road. He opened the disinfectant, cleaned my arm, and hit the vein the very first time. I didn't even fill the stick.

When we arrived, I remember looking out the back of the ambulance at the lights of the city. My family was following closely behind.

As we pulled up to the hospital, I started feeling really dizzy. As the paramedic pulled me out of the ambulance I remember grabbing his arm and saying, "Oh no, it's happening again." I felt my spirit leave my body. It felt like I was literally floating in the air. I had never had such an experience before that night.

Chapter 4

THE NIGHTMARE BEGINS

At the hospital they rushed me into the emergency room and began working with me. I felt like I was on a fast roller coaster. They hooked me up to a heart monitor and gave me medicine. My heart kept speeding out of control. As my family came running into the room I heard the nurses say, "It seems to be her heart."

They moved me to a better equipped section where there were more monitors and the CAT scan machine. It wasn't long till my sister-in-law, JoAnn, and her husband, Junior, arrived. Pastor Frank from our church also came. Joni stayed by my side. She kept asking "Are you OK? You looked as white as a sheet in the ambulance. Do you want me to call your parents in Arlington?"

"No." I replied. "My mom has just got out of the hospital with high blood pressure and my dad has just had surgery. He came home last night. Besides I will be out by morning." I told my husband, "I am OK. Can you go get Jimmy Alan?" I wanted his father to be the one who told him I was in the hospital, lest he should panic.

All I wanted them to do was to find out what was wrong with me so I could go home. I never thought one time that I was so close to death. I honestly thought I was pregnant and my pituitary gland was enlarged causing this reaction. I had told Joni that I had been really tired lately, so that was the first thing we asked the nurses to check. One nurse told me that pregnancy could have nothing to do with my heart, but she would check with the doctors.

Finally the doctor came in and said, "We are going to put her into CCU. May I see her chart to see if she is stable enough to be moved?" The nurses kept their eyes fixed on the monitor at all times, and my family took turns by my side.

It seemed like I was in the emergency room a long time before they came to get me. I remember asking Joni, "Why do I have to go to CCU? That's for people who are really sick. I don't fit into that category." Soon they came and took me to CCU. This was Saturday, October 17 at about 10:30 p.m.

Between Saturday night and Sunday morning I grew progressively worse. They had to shock me every five to fifteen minutes all night long. With my family by my side I often could hear Joni scream, "Donna, you have to breathe."

Fear filled the room. The pain was unbearable. The nurses would shock me and then shake my arm, trying to get me to breathe. I felt myself floating up and I could see my body jerking and even hear the nurses' voices. It felt like a magnet was pulling me up and another magnet was pulling me back down. We fought for life all night long. I put on the armor of God and got ready for battle.

Put on the whole armor of God, that ye may be able to stand against the wiles of the devil (Eph. 6:11 KJV).

I rebuked Satan every time I went up and I praised God every time I came down. I knew Satan was trying to destroy the good works I was trying to do for our Lord. I wanted people to know about Jesus, what he had done for me in the past, and what he was going to do in my future. I lay there almost lifeless, praying and saying that fear wasn't of the Lord. I knew the Lord didn't give me the spirit of fear.

For God hath not given us the spirit of fear; but of power, and of love, and of a sound mind (2 Tim.1:7 KJV).

I still fought this fear every step of the way. This was a spiritual war and the battle was the Lord's.

And all this assembly shall know that the LORD saveth not with sword and spear: for the battle is the LORD'S, and he will give you into our hands (1 Sam. 17:47 KJV).

Satan puts obstacles and circumstances in our way to get our eyes off of God. It's time we put our finger under the nose of the devil and say what the Bible says. Let's invade devil's territory and take back what he has stolen from us. Everyone was prepared to pray and speak until this sickness lined up with the Word of God. Satan didn't have a chance.

I knew I would be victorious either way. If it was my time to go, I would wake up in Daddy God's arms; if not, he would heal me because his Word promised he would. We prayed and prayed, but as the night went on, I grew worse. That was the hardest night of my life hearing those awful machines going off and knowing that I was going to be shocked during the fight for my life.

The next morning my pastor and my husband's pastor came to check on me before church. Sonya Shepard, a friend from Bethel Temple, brought me a cassette with healing Scriptures and healing praises, telling me to listen to them nonstop. JoAnn brought me her cassette player with earphones. I couldn't wait to put the tape in and listen to it. She also brought my favorite tape called Nana's Tape that she had made with her favorite songs on it. I loved it. They put the earphones on my head, and I listened to the Scriptures even as they were shocking me. This could fill me with the Word of God and I needed to be healed.

Many people from our church came, and everyone was praying. That morning I told Joni to call my parents. I knew if they were not called, they would be upset with me, but when they were called, they would come immediately. My mom's blood pressure might go "sky high," but they still needed to know.

They still had to shock me every few minutes. I was getting worried, but I tried not to show it. However, I began to wonder if something was really wrong with my heart. After hearing the nurses all night long, my faith was growing weak. People were there to lift me up and tell me they loved me and that no matter the circumstances, we were standing on God's Word. Satan wanted me to let my guard down so he could attack full force. As long as I was listening to God's Word, he had no power, but as soon as I started doubting, he could come in like a roaring lion. I tried so hard.

Every time I started thinking I might die I just said, "I rebuke you Satan."

Be sober, be vigilant; because your adversary the devil, as a roaring lion, walketh about, seeking whom he may devour (1 Peter 5:8 KJV).

Then the Lord would fill the room with peace.

I had assumed I would be out of the hospital before Sunday, but after the Saturday night's anxiety, Jimmy and Joni decided to call my parents. Within two hours my parents, Bill and Edith Harris, my sister Shelly, my brother Mike, and the rest of my family finally arrived from Arlington. I got to see them for a few minutes. I just wanted to reassure them that I was going to be fine, and let them all know how much I loved them.

Then, about 11:30 a.m. on Sunday morning, I went into code blue. They had shocked me twice and were doing manual CPR on me, but I was not responding. They turned up the machine and shocked me again and again as I floated toward the ceiling. I could see and hear everything in the room and the frantic look on everyone faces. The nurses and doctors were running around. My body was jerking up off the bed every time they shocked me. I was floating above my body, watching them. I heard the nurses say, "She can't take much more. We have to let her go."

As they frantically started pushing Joni out of the room, I could hear her fighting with them. She was screaming, "She will listen to me. Donna will listen to me! You have to let me stay." As they forced her down the hall and as my spirit floated up toward the brightest light, she screamed, "Donna you have to breathe now! Donna! Donna, breathe!"

Who only hath immortality, dwelling in the light which no man can approach unto; whom no man hath seen, nor can see: to whom be honor and power everlasting. Amen (1 Tim. 6:16 KJV).

It was the brightest light I had ever seen. It was brighter than the sun yet it was warm and didn't hurt my eyes. As I passed, these figures were glowing. I couldn't make out faces, only bodies. I just knew they were angels. The main thing I remember about them is just the love I felt. And above them I saw large hands reaching out for me as I was reaching out for our Lord. I felt like I was on my tiptoes giving all the strength that I had left in my body to reach him. What I felt was love and awesome peace and indescribable sweetness. My niece told me later that they had said that I had a blank stare on my face and that I was gone. To be absent from the body is to be with the Lord.

We are confident, I say, and willing rather to be absent from the body, and to be present with the Lord (2 Cor.5:8 KJV).

I could no longer see anyone in the room only above me. Right before our hands were about to touch I heard Joni scream again, "You have to breath now!" She was crying with a sound of desperation. She screamed at the top of her lungs, "Donna, breathe," and I gasped for air. I felt a magnet pull me back down into my body.

And her spirit came again, and she arose straightway: and he commanded to give her meat. (Luke 8:55) They tied me down and crammed tubes down my throat. Since my veins had collapsed, they cut a three-port central line on the left side of my chest and a single port on the right. They put in a pacemaker and put me on a respirator. I was now on total life support. Satan thought at this point he had won the battle. He had me on total life support with tubes down my throat so I couldn't rebuke him anymore. He did not know, however, that I had people who loved me and were willing to stand in the gap for me. They would be my voice and my strength. They would stand and cry out to our father for me. One by one, they went to the throne room of God for me.

Let us therefore come boldly unto the throne of grace that we may obtain mercy, and find grace to help in time of need (Heb. 4:16 KJV).

Chapter 5

SEEMS TO BE HER HEART

The doctor came out to talk to the family and said, "Donna is very serious. We have tried everything. She is on the three strongest rhythm drugs in the world and she is not responding. We have nothing else available. We might be able to do a heart transplant if and when she is stabilized, but right now she too critical and she can't be moved." Then he told my husband, "If she does wake up, there will be a high chance of her being brain-dead. I think it might be a virus that has attacked her heart."

The fear that filled the waiting room was unbearable. Everyone was crying. They told the doctors that there has to be something else that could be done. Maybe another doctor from another hospital could help. The doctor got upset because he didn't want to call in anyone else. He told my family he was the best. But they were very persistent, they wanted a second opinion. So he called Baylor Hospital. My parents had a lot of faith in that hospital because of a Christian doctor that my mom had when she had cancer. He always stated that he prays for his patients, so that is where they called. The heart specialist he talked to told him they would do the same thing that the Abilene doctor was doing. Our next step was just to wait. My family was not ready to give up. They were depending on a Greater Physician.

Joni and JoAnn had bulldog faith. As Joni sat by my side, JoAnn went into the waiting room and said to everyone there, "We are depending on a Greater Physician; if you can't talk life with God's words, not death, then don't go into the room. We only want people who believe just like we do around us. We don't need any unbelievers bringing doubt into the room."

Death and life are in the power of the tongue: and they that love it shall eat the fruit thereof (Prov.18:21 KJV).

We know what the Bible says and we believe our Lord will come through. When we have done all that we know to do, we will just stand and wait.

We can bear anything as long as we know that you remain strong in him (1 Thess.3:8 LIVING).

As I slowly opened my eyes, I noticed it was 1:00 p.m. I remember looking around and wondering where all the wires came from and why I was tied down. Oh, what joy filled my heart to see my family by my side. They seemed as happy to see me as I was to see them. What a journey of lights I had traveled on. With the tubes down my throat I couldn't talk. I learned to point at what I needed. My body would feel really cold then I would get extremely hot. The nurses said that was because of all the machines I was hooked up to. My niece could look at my eyes and know if I needed the blanket on or off. I tried to write but with all the IV's running everywhere I couldn't.

Finally, I looked up and here came Jimmy, my husband. It seemed like it had been a long time since I had seen him. He had the waiting room ministry. He couldn't stand to see me in so much pain. Our whole church family, he and many others, spent their time in the chapel praying for me as well as others in the CCU. At one point there were probably two hundred people standing in faith just for me.

Again I say unto you, that if two of you shall agree on earth as touching any thing that they shall ask, it shall be done for them of my Father which is in heaven. For where two or three are gathered together in my name, there am I in the midst of them (Matt. 18:19-20 KJV).

Our pastor got permission and brought in my two oldest children, Jimmy Alan and Chris. The look on their faces when they saw me was almost unbearable. I told them with my fingers that I loved them and

I would be OK. I had not cried since I was in the hospital. I had to be focused and strong. As my husband and my children left the room, the tears began to flow. Joni held me for the longest time. That was when I noticed how close to death I truly was.

Chapter 6

TOTAL LIFE
SUPPORT, NO HOPE

Every few minutes all day long they still had to shock me. They would shock me to get my heart back in control and then scream for me to breathe. After a long day of fighting for my life, I was getting weaker with each passing moment. With trembling hands I wrote a note asking, "Joni, how many times?" I wanted to know how many times they had shocked me, because it seemed like every couple minutes that awful machine would go off.

Joni responded, "I think about twenty-seven."

All day Sunday many people came to pray for me. People we didn't even know asked if they could pray. One lady gave Joni a book on God's promises. She read it to me over and over when I wasn't listening to my tapes.

We had a family from our church take in our three boys with Christian love. Joni and Billy had Daniel, Tiffany, and youngest, Brandon, was seven years old.

Joni rarely left my side. We made sure our children were born close to the same time so they always had someone their age to play with. She is closer than a sister. I always knew what she was thinking. Through the bad times and good times, we have been there for each other. She told the nurses I was the other half of her heart. We are very close.

Some of the people that came to see me were talking death. My heart raced when I heard what they were saying. I may not have looked like I was going to live, with all my wires and tubes, but I was, I just knew it. Joni watched the monitor at all times, and when she saw the fear in my eyes she told them leave the room. The look on my face told the story. I couldn't believe someone could be so inconsiderate. They were worried about the burial cost. If I could have talked, I would have thrown them out myself. I wanted to scream, *I will live and I will not die!*

The pain was almost unbearable. They continued shocking me every few minutes. As the sun set, I had made it through the day. I had many visitors all day long. James and Lori Kilpatrick from Bethel Temple had come to see me. Barry and Kim had anointed me with oil and prayed for me.

Is any sick among you? Let him call for the elders of the church; and let them pray over him, anointing him with oil in the name of the Lord (James 5:14 KJV).

Pastor Frank, Ivelene, and Sister Sonya, came by to check on me. Many people were in and out. My strength was fading fast. People from work came by, even my boy's pediatrician dropped in. They told me I needed to rest so I tried to sleep, but with the tubes down my throat and all the wires, I couldn't. I motioned for my tape so I could try to relax. I put it in and I listened. Even though I had fought for my life all day, I still had such peace. I knew this must be the peace beyond understanding the Bible talked about.

If you do this, you will experience God's peace, which is far more wonderful than the human mind can understand. And the peace of God, which passeth all understanding, shall keep your hearts and minds through Christ Jesus (Phil. 4:7 KJV).

I knew I was victorious either way; if it was my time to go I would wake up in Daddy God's arms. If not, he would heal me. His Word promised he would, so I fought for life and waited.

At about 8:30 p.m., my sister-in-law and brother-in-law had to go home. They hadn't left the hospital since I had been put in the night before. I waved bye as they walked out the door.

My physical body was going down, but my spiritual body was rising with the greatest strength that pours down from the throne of God.

But they that wait upon the LORD shall renew their strength; they shall mount up with wings as eagles; they shall run, and not be weary; and they shall walk, and not faint (Isa. 40:31 KJV).

All our prayers were being heard. About 8:45 p.m., my sister-in-law and brother-in-law arrived home to find my nephew Daniel kneeling beside their bed. He was praying for me. He was going straight to the thrown room for me, crying out. He knew the pain that I felt; he had a central line just like I did. He had leukemia when he was little and our Lord had come through and healed him. He was pleading for my healing. JoAnn joined him by the bed; both them were in desperate prayer. Finally, JoAnn got up and walked across the room and said, "Lord it says in your Word you will never put more on someone than they can handle. Lord Donna's had enough!"

For he will not lay upon man more than right; that he should enter into judgment with God (Job 34:23 KJV).

PRAYERS HEARD

The time was 9:00 p.m. Sunday night. At that very moment, that same hour, my heart came in alignment with God's Word. I didn't know that JoAnn and Daniel had prayed for me that night, but I knew it had been fifteen minutes and I hadn't been shocked. Then I noticed that it had been thirty minutes, then three hours. As the night went on, the more excited I got. Every time I heard the machines in the other rooms going off Joni would just say, "That's not you, honey. That's not you."

I just praised God, "Thank you Holy Father." I knew finally he was coming through. Through the night I never had to be shocked again.

As I lay there listening to my tape, I heard *There is a way when you think you cannot make it. There is a way when you think you cannot take it, this very day.* There is a way with the Lord. There is a peace that passeth all understanding. We have a God that can lift his mighty hand and make us a way when there was none before. Then he said, *If you diligently harken to the voice of the Lord and obey his commandments he will not let diseases come on you. For I am the Lord your God that healeth you.* As I lay there quietly praising God for bringing me this far, something marvelous happened.

I looked up and I felt a warm, peaceful feeling. Then I saw the brightest light. The same light I had seen when I had floated up earlier that day, brighter than looking into the sun—illuminating. Then I felt the Lord's presence. As I looked up, I saw an image of the Lord from the top of his head to the bottom of his feet. Then, like fireworks, I saw his face in all four corners of the room. He was smiling at me.

Then the Lord descended in the form of a pillar of cloud and stood there with him, and passed in front of him and announced the meaning of his name. "I am Jehovah, the merciful and gracious God," he said, "slow to anger and rich in steadfast love and Truth (Ex.34:5Living).

I lay there almost in anticipation for what he had for me next. After seeing the vision of the Lord, I felt a love like I had never experienced in my life. This was so much more than any human love, so much more than we are able to give or receive in our life time. This was a heavenly love from our Father of Lights.

Every good gift and every perfect gift is from above, and cometh down from the Father of Lights, with whom is no variableness, neither shadow of turning (James 1:17 KJV).

I started praising him like never before. My spirit fell to my knees. "Oh, thank you, Lord that you're going to heal me. Thank you, Lord Jesus that you're going to change me. Thank you, Lord that you're going to fill my cup to overflowing."

Lord, I am overflowing with your blessings, just as you promised (Ps. 119:65 LIVING).

"Oh thank you, Lord for your holy presence and your anointing on this place. Oh Father God, thank you for putting my family, who love you as much as I do, into my path. The ones willing to stand in the gap for me and hold me up when I am too weak to stand, the mighty army you sent to be bold and by my side my every waking moment," and on and on I prayed. "Praise you, Jesus." I lay there in such reverence. The tears fell down my cheek as I was in his presence waiting for what was next.

Then I saw the horse, a great white stallion galloping as fast as he could go and on his back was our Lord. I saw red drops on his garment as it flew behind him. He had a two-edged sword out of his mouth. Coming swiftly as the wind were demons headed straight for him, moving fast like a strobe light. But before they could get into the presence of the light, they fell off. The words of God we were quoting were fighting for us. We had been rebuking those demons from the first day I was in the hospital. We knew God and his words would fight this fight. This was the fight of faith.

> And I saw heaven opened, and behold a white horse; and he that sat upon him was called Faithful and True, and in righteousness he doth judge and make war. His eyes were as a flame of fire, and on his head were many crowns; and he had a name written, that no man knew, but he himself. And he was clothed with a vesture dipped in blood: and his name is called The Word of God. And the armies which were in heaven followed him upon white horses, clothed in fine linen, white and clean. And out of his mouth goeth a sharp sword, that with it he should smite the nations: and he shall rule them with a rod of iron: and he treadeth the winepress of the fierceness and wrath of Almighty God.And he hath on his vesture and on his thigh a name written, KING OF KINGS, AND LORD OF LORDS.
>
> (Rev. 19:11-16 KJV)

That's why we stood so firm on Scripture. Every thing the Bible says we can have is ours. We found my healing in the Scriptures and waited on our Lord to deliver. He always answers his Word. His Word says he will never leave us or forsake us. We knew he was in total control.

The next thing that happened showed me how much he truly loved me—how much he truly loves all of us. A healing light fell from heaven and landed directly on my heart. It was warm. It felt like someone with huge hands was hugging me. I was lying flat on the bed yet these hands were under me.

But whatever is good and perfect comes to us from God, the Creator of all light, and he shines forever without change or shadow (James 1:17 LIVING).

The priests have to go outside because the glory of the Lord is filling the entire building! (1 Kings 8:11 LIVING).

I knew at that point I was going to be OK. I knew that I had been healed. The circumstance didn't look like it; I had the pain of all the tubes and felt the burns all over my chest. I was still hooked up to all the life support. But I knew everything wasn't always as it seemed in the natural, especially now.

Chapter 8

HEART CAME INTO ALIGNMENT WITH GOD'S WORD

All day Monday I continue to improve. I couldn't wait for them to take out the tubes so I could share everything our Lord God had shown me. I struggled to write but I just couldn't. I listened to my tapes and had many visitors.

Armida Sewell came in to see me. I was so worn out from the day before, I went in and out of consciousness most of the day. She left me a note to read as soon as I was able. It said, "Donna, please rest and let your healing manifest. Don't listen to any negative talk or confessions. Donna, talk to our Lord Jesus with your mind and heart. There are angels posted here with you. Don't be afraid only believe."

What is it then? I will pray with the spirit, and I will pray with the understanding also: I will sing with the spirit, and I will sing with the understanding also (1 Cor.14:15 KJV).

My spirit was soaring high as a giant eagle but my flesh was extremely weak.

But they that wait upon the Lord shall renew their strength. They shall mount up with wings like eagles; they shall run and not be weary; they shall walk and not faint (Isa. 40:31 KJV).

I was fighting with every ounce of strength that I had left in my body just to stay awake, but no matter how hard I tried, I just couldn't.

Tuesday morning at 5:30 a.m., I was experiencing pain unlike I'd ever felt my whole life. I kept feeling like I couldn't breathe and was going to drown. With the tubes down my throat, I couldn't swallow, cough, or speak. I felt helpless. The nurse came in when she saw me desperately moving around. I motioned toward my tube. She knew by the gargling sounds it needed to be suctioned. She quickly proceeded to get all the equipment together. The pain was excruciating when they suctioned out my tube. This procedure had to be done several times during the night, but afterwards I felt better. As they started to work on me, the doctor came in and said, "Nurse, let me see her chart. Wow! She did well all night long so let's just take it out." I was so excited. Finally I would be able to speak.

Tuesday morning at about sunrise I saw the bright light. Again, I felt the presence of God fill the room. His presence is where my strength came from, it continued to chase away all my fear.

In the day when I cried thou answeredst me, and strengthenst me with strength in my soul (Ps. 138:3 KJV).

As the tears flowed down my cheeks and hit the pillow, I saw a cloud in the room it had these words written inside it: "I can do all things through Christ which strengtheneth me (Phil.4:13 KJV). I knew this was Philippians 4:13. This was the Lord's way of telling me I'm with you and I'll never leave you. I felt so loved. Then another cloud had written in it, "You will come back seventy thousand times stronger."

These words came at the exact time I needed them. Now I was armed and ready for the battle of one more day. He then told me *Donna, you will write a book I've shown you with Scripture.* I could hardly believe what I heard. I didn't even pay attention in English class in school and spelling wasn't my best subject. So, I knew if I was to write a book it would definitely be God. But I knew what I heard was my Father's voice, and it would come to pass.

And a stranger will they not follow, but will flee from him: for they know not the voice of strangers (John 10:5 KJV).

I quickly pointed at a sheet of paper on my tray. The nurse handed it to me. I wanted to write everything the Lord had shown me down. That way I wouldn't forget any part. I wrote on everything I could get my hands on.

The doctor came in and told my family, "The angiogram is scheduled for this morning at 7:30 a.m. We need to find out how much damage she has. We have shocked her forty-one times in the last twenty-four hours. I'm not sure what we will find. It's medically impossible for her not to have some redness or damage; so get prepared; she will have some. We just don't know how extensive her injuries may be."

I had come so far I wasn't looking back now, only forward. I knew the great things the Lord was about to do. Soon I would be able to share everything the Lord had shown me with the ones I love.

The doctor came back in to talk to me. I was slowly getting my voice back. I tried to speak, but nothing came out, so I wrote down on a piece of paper, "You will find no damage. I am healed. Our Lord God healed me."

The look on the doctor's face was one of unbelief. I knew what the doctor's prognosis was, but I still knew the truth. I couldn't wait for them to take me to the procedure room where I could prove that our Lord God had come through and healed me just like his Word promised he would do.

Finally, it was 7:30 a.m. The nurse was right on time. They walked in and asked me if I was ready to go. I responded by saying yes. I was so ready to get out of this room, even if it was just down the hall. As they pushed me down the hall, JoAnn and Junior showed up. My voice had come back so JoAnn and I began to sing praises to my Lord and King, "You are beautiful beyond description, too marvelous for words. Too wonderful for comprehension, like nothing ever seen or heard. Who can grasp your infinite wisdom? Who can fathom the depths of your love? You are beautiful beyond description, majesty enthroned above." With everything that was in me I sang at the top of my lungs, "I stand, I stand in awe of you. I stand, I stand in awe of you. Holy Lord to whom all praise is due, I stand in awe of you!"

Then they pushed me into the room, and I lay there just waiting. I told the nurses, "You will find no damage because our Lord God has totally healed me." Then I continued to sing until they took me into the procedure room. I kept telling the doctors about our Lord and how he does heal today and how it was for anyone who believed. Jesus saves all.

They kept trying to put me to sleep, but no matter how much medicine they gave me, I continued to preach and sing to them.

The nurses asked, "How are you?"

I responded by saying, "I have never been better." In all the years of doing procedures in that room, never had anyone ever responded that way. I was so joyful and I had a love for everyone like never before.

We know how much God loves us because we have felt his love and because we believe him when he tells us that he loves us dearly. God is love, and anyone who lives in love is living with God and God is living in him (1 John 4:16 LIVING).

I kept telling them how blessed I was to be there and how great our God was. I asked them, "If you find no damage will you then believe?"

Suddenly, the doctor that was working on me got really quiet. Then, I heard him say, "Check again, this can't be. Nurse, get the dye. This just can't be."

Even with the dye they found exactly what I had said, "No redness and absolutely no damage." I lay there, finally quiet, and just smiled. I had already said all that needed to be said. Not only had our Lord healed my old heart, he had given me a complete new heart.

And I will give you a new heart – I will give you new and right desires and put a new spirit within you. I will take out your stony hearts of sin and give you new hearts of love (Ezek. 36:26 LIVING).

What a wonderful God we have. Oh, how I exalt the Lord for his healing power and grace. By his stripes I am healed. Our Lord God is so worthy of our praise!

Now, not even the doctors could deny the healing power of our Lord. They heard it, saw it, and still didn't believe it. As they stood there, desperately searching and still finding no damage, the doctor told the nurse, "Go ahead and take her into recovery."

Chapter 9

COMING BACK

A s they pushed me into recovery, I could hardly wait to see my family. Even though the doctor didn't tell me they had not found any damage, I knew. I just sang to the nurses and praised God. I told everyone in there, "By his stripes I am healed." It seemed like I was in recovery a very long time. I told everyone in there about our Lord Jesus.

JoAnn and Junior left to visit a friend of theirs who was in the hospital. He had to have some tests done on his heart that same morning. When they entered his room, he was talking about this woman who was down in the recovery room. He told them that the doctors said that he was going to need triple by pass surgery done on his heart and he said, "I was so afraid. But there was this woman, she was singing in the recovery room this morning and telling everyone about Jesus and how he had healed her. She wasn't even talking to me, but such a peace filled that room. It's so hard to explain but, I'm no longer afraid."

Junior and JoAnn sat there quietly then she said, "Oh, I know who that was, that is my sister-in-law Donna. The Lord had healed her heart. She was on total life support and the doctors gave very little hope. They wanted to do a heart transplant but she was too unstable to be moved. We thank the Lord, she came back as fast as she left. We do have a healing Jesus! We had better go and get back before the doctor comes to talk to the family."

Shortly after they arrived downstairs the doctor came in. He needed to talk to the family. With an overwhelmed look on his face he said, "I can't explain this. It goes against all of my teaching on the human body. We honestly thought it was medically impossible. People normally can't be shocked forty-one times and not have some kind of redness or damage. We didn't know how extensive her damage would be but we knew she would have some. She told us there would be no damage and we found absolutely what she had said, 'No damage, even with the dye.'" The doctor still looking very puzzled, shook his head, and left the room.

My family knew our Lord had come through. We had stood firm on the Word of God. The sadness of the last few days was finally over. Everyone was hugging and giving God the glory—great things he had done. The Lord's presence filled all who were in the waiting room.

I returned back to my room totally exhausted. The medicine finally started to work. I smiled at my family and asked for my tape; then I fell fast to sleep. This was the deepest sleep I'd ever had.

Later that evening I remember waking up and finding my family by my side. I was so excited my voice had come back. Now I could tell them about the journey of lights and the messages the Lord had given me. I hugged Joni and Jimmy and one-by-one, I got to see the whole family and tell them all how much I loved them. I talked so fast they had to slow me down. I had so much to share. I knew my family would believe me.

The nurses would often come in the room. One nurse named Janie told me the presence of God was so strong in that room she just wanted to stay in there. I ministered to her a lot. I looked forward to shift changes, even the maid mopping the floor. I told everyone who got close to my room about Jesus.

I had many visitors and people praying for me. My room was very busy. I was so happy to see my sons and tell them I loved them and I was OK. You should never let a day go by that you don't tell the ones you love how you feel. Time is too short.

All day Wednesday I continued to improve. The whole hospital was talking about the healing in CCU. I listened to my tapes until the battery ran out and asked for more. I would read what the Lord had given me over and over again. I even drew pictures in the dark.

Soon I had some more visitors come in. They were called the Prayer Warriors. They were members of a local church in my city. They had heard I was really bad and they came to pray for me. There were ten of them, but they could only visit three at a time. They were praying for all the families in CCU. As they entered the room they felt the presence of the Lord. They started smiling and looking around. One of the men said, "The presence of God is so strong in this room. WOW!" They asked me if they could pray for me.

I replied, "Yes," as they opened the large bottle of holy oil to anoint me with. They started at my feet.

I said, "I would love your prayers but before you pray, let me tell you what our Lord Jesus has done for me." I went into how our Lord had healed me. They just started dancing around the room practically screaming, "Praise God! Praise God! Hallelujah!" I wanted to dance to but the nurses wouldn't let me out of the bed. Before they left I prayed for them and we had church right there in CCU.

When the first three went out and another group came in, two men and a woman. They wanted to hear the whole story how our Lord had healed me. I proceeded to share with them. Finally, they told me that they had been praying for people all day long and shared about a demon possessed man who had been delivered that very night. He had accepted Jesus and burned all his hard rock music. I rejoiced with them. I prayed for them and they left praising God all the way down the hall.

It was getting late so I asked to see Jimmy. As he came in, he kissed me on the forehead and told me, "Honey, you have had a busy day; you need your rest." I got a big hug and a kiss then I praised God and went to sleep. Joni finally left my side today and went home. I assured her I would be OK.

Chapter 10

TOTALLY HEALED

The Lord had sent many angels to be by my side through this time.

The angel of the LORD encamped round about them that fear him, and delivered them (Ps. 34:7 KJV).

There was a woman who came up to Joni and gave her a book on God's promises. There was a gray-haired man that prayed for the family and was only seen one time. The nurse I had on Wednesday was my friend's brother that I hadn't seen since 1978. We spent half the night talking about old times, praising God together. He told me you that can't be in this kind of business and not believe in miracles and Jesus. He had seen many people healed and told me several stories. Then he left the room so I could try to get some rest, but I was so excited I couldn't. I started praising our God again and just thanking him for the wonderful messages he had given to me. I pulled out my papers that I had written on what the Lord had given to me so far and read them over and over again. I felt like dancing but I just couldn't get out of the bed.

I lay there in awe just to think how much our Lord loves us. The love is so much more than our human minds can ever conceive in our lifetime—more powerful than a mother with a new born baby. As I lay there praising our Lord, I felt his presence. What a glorious feeling. I had felt it before as I praised Jesus. Somehow, now I knew I was closer to it. I could hear the Lord's voice like I had never heard it before.

The peace and glory of his presence filled my every waking moment. My spiritual ears were open to every word he spoke. As the light filled the room, I saw his face. I smiled and got my pen ready for what he was going to tell me.

Chapter 11

DONNA, IT IS YOU!

As I lay there quietly, I felt such a peace. The anointing fell on the room like a warm fog. The presence of our God Almighty is so powerful. As I lay there, he started showing me things. I wrote quickly to receive everything he told me word-for-word.

The next thing I saw was my church. It was packed with people and I was a worship leader. People were getting out of wheelchairs; arms were growing out were there were none. Everyone was happy and dancing. The pastor was swinging his wife around. There were angels in both corners and a golden rainbow in the back of the room.

I do set my bow in the cloud, and it shall be for a token of a covenant between me and the earth (Gen. 9:13 KJV).

He gave me messages for different people in my church. One of the messages showed a tightrope and this woman was high in the air, walking very slowly. In a second she began to fall. She fell for a long time it seemed, and then this hand came up from nowhere and caught her. She bounced as if in a cloud. Then the Lord said, *Sometimes you have to fall, that way I can bring you up to the level I need you at.*

As I lay there in anticipation, the Lord showed me this woman. She was in a large arena packed with people all the way to the ceiling. There was a big church with a huge stage and lots of steps. She was pacing back and forth, back and forth. I noticed that people were again getting out of wheel chairs and cancers were falling off in the floor. Many different kinds of healing were happening all at once. I asked the Lord, "Who is she? Lord, who is she?"

As I lay there it was like the Lord opened the windows of my spirit and took a mirror and held it up to my face and said, *Donna, it is you.*

The tears rolled down my cheeks I was so overwhelmed with emotion, I felt like I didn't deserve all his splendor and glory. But because of his awesome love and grace he was still going to give me the desires of my heart and use me for his glory.

I couldn't wait for what was next. I knew tomorrow I was going to get to go to PCU. Finally, I would be able to get out of the bed and talk to everyone the Lord sends me to. As I wrote, my hands never got tired. The Lord spoke to me in such a way I heard his voice in my spirit. It was so very clear and I knew it was my Father's voice.

My sheep hear my voice, and I know them, and they follow me (John 10:27 KJV).

STILL LOOKING FOR AN EXPLANATION

Thursday morning they wanted to do an electro study on my heart to try to find out why this had happened. They were still searching for the reason my heart did this. They also wanted to put in a defibrillator. I asked the Lord, "Lord you totally healed me. Why must I have a defibrillator?"

What I heard was, *In three years they will turn it off and do some testing. When they still find no damage then I will get the glory.* So I decided to let them put the defibrillator in. I knew tomorrow would be a busy day so I quickly fell asleep.

Early Thursday morning I woke up. I asked the time and it was 5:30 a.m. I had been blessed with another day and opportunity to share Jesus with everyone that came in the room. I got my pen back out just in case there was more from God that I didn't get last night. I knew our Lord would bring it back into my remembrance. Soon the Lord showed me a green army helicopter. There were two people in it. Below them were brown and black straw huts. They were handing food and blankets down to millions of people. The people looked as though they were hungry. They all had their hands raised to receive as they slowly sat the food on the ground. I knew our Lord was trying to tell me something but I didn't understand. I asked the Lord if it was me and he never confirmed.

Then he showed me a large building it looked like an embassy. There were a man and lady standing down at the end of this long hall. She was short and had dark hair and the man was heavy built. People were lined up, and as they came, the couple was kissing them on each cheek and opening the door for them to go in. To this day I don't know what the Lord was trying to tell me, but I know in the right timing I will know all—all in the Lord's timing. I feel that someone I know will be a missionary in another country. I really don't know who, but somehow I don't feel like it will be me.

Soon the doctor came in to tell me about the electro study. He said, "We will speed your heart up and then slow it down where we can study it. We need to find the reason your heart did this. Then we will put in the defibrillator. This will be a two hour surgery." They left the room to talk to the family. The doctors explained what was going to take place. Soon they came to get me and I again told them our Lord had totally healed me, and I had a brand new heart. I sang all the way down the hall. Soon I would be able to run the halls.

First, the doctor who was to do the electro study on my heart started shocking my heart. He was trying to make it stop, trying to make it speed up or even slow down, but my heart continued to beat regularly, just like our Lord God had designed it to. No matter what they did to it, they couldn't get it off its rhythm. Finally, the doctor gave up. Shaking his head, he told the other doctor, "It's time to put in the defibrillator." They got the surgery done in twenty minutes and sent me to recovery, praising our Lord.

The doctor came back in to talk to the family. He started by saying, "We can't explain this but we couldn't get her heart to do any thing but beat."

The other doctor said he had never put in a defibrillator so easily before. It was a textbook case. "All I had to do was cut her open and set it right in. Everything vein was right in the exact place it needed to be." Then he concluded by saying, "I've done a lot of these procedures and never once have I seen anything like this."

My family told them that describes our healing Jesus. What is impossible with man are always possible with our God.

PCU

They took me to recovery and then back into my room. My family was waiting for me to tell me what the doctor had said, but I already knew they wouldn't find any damage to my heart. We had doubled up on prayer and we were ready for anything. We had all been in the presence of God, and that is where our strength comes from. When the Holy Spirit moves in on a situation, he does it with wisdom and understanding so vast that it staggers the human mind. The Holy Spirit is the muscle of God. Every time you see God's power in manifestation you can be sure the Holy Spirit is on the scene. We had already seen the power of the Lord. I wasn't anticipating what he had for us next.

I was so excited, this was the day I got to go to PCU. I would be able to walk the halls and tell everyone about how our Lord Jesus had healed me. I had many visitors come in to see me. My friends and family kept me busy visiting, so the time went quickly. I told everyone what the Lord had shown me so far. I had no doubt that it would all come to pass.

Finally, the nurse came in and said, "We are going to take the IV out today and we will be moving you to PCU soon." I could hardly wait. It seemed like I had been in the hospital forever.

As they were getting me ready to go to PCU, another doctor came in from the burn unit to check my burns from that awful machine. She introduced herself and said, "Did you know you are lucky to be alive? People usually don't live after what you've been through."

"Yes, but I know the Greater Physician. Our Lord God is the one that gave me the strength and desire to keep on fighting," I told her. I knew he would heal me. That is what the Bible said. He took the stripes on his back for our healing. By his stripes I am healed.

But he was wounded for our transgressions; he was bruised for our iniquities: the chastisement of our peace was upon him; and with his stripes we are healed (Isa. 53:5 KJV).

She just smiled and continued to put gel on my burns. They looked like third or fourth degree burns. I told her that these burns are just a tiny reminder of the pain our Lord had gone through on the cross. "He died for us you know?"

She said, "Yes, I do know."

"These burns will heal really fast too. The Lord said, 'I'm healed of everything that Satan had tried to put on me and that's how I know I will heal fast."

She quickly finished her work, wished me luck, and told me good-bye.

The other nurse had come back into the room to take out my IV. "Your room is almost ready," she said. "We have to get you ready too, OK?"

Sonya Madison, a friend from church was waiting outside of the room to see me. She was the song leader at Bethel Temple. I had wanted to see her since I had been put in the hospital. I knew she would believe everything I told her and be another one to praise God for the miracle of life he had given me. She is another special friend.

As the nurse unhooked the heart monitor, she noticed it was still going. She kept watching it, waiting for it to flat line, but it just kept on beating just like my heart. Stunned, she asked, "How long has that heart monitor been going?"

"For a while," I said. "I have been watching it also. I knew it was unhooked. Nothing surprises me about our Lord. Now, what church do you go to?"

I felt she thought I was not human. I watched the monitor, thanked the Lord, and laughed as it finally flat lined. Finally, the IV was out and

I got to get up and get into the wheelchair. It felt good to be out of that bed. The nurse opened the curtain and everyone came in. We were ready to go to my new room. They pushed me to the elevator and into my room. The first thing I noticed was the special camera above the television in my room. It was placed there to watch me. I guess they thought I was still sick. Everyone walked into my room. I was so happy to be out of bed. I stood up and looked around, suddenly realizing what I had been through I started hugging and dancing with everyone in the room. Finally the nightmares of the earlier days were coming to an end.

Chapter 14

PROPHESY WAS TOLD

My friends soon left so I could rest a little, but all I wanted to do was get out of the bed and walk the halls. I went to make me some coffee, and I met the head nurse. She was a Baptist preacher's wife and I told her about the healing and how thankful I was to be alive. I give my Lord Jesus all of the glory for the great things he has done. We stood there and talked for a long time. She was captivated by my every word. Soon I was tired and decided to go back to my room. Within an hour the nurses were lined up down the hall to talk to me and I ministered to them all. They'd heard about the person getting healed and wanted all the details. One by one, I told them of God's glory and grace. I talked to everyone who even came close to the room. If too much time went by without someone coming in, I would go into the waiting room just to share our wonderful Jesus. He had given me the gift of life and I wanted everyone to know about it.

Soon, my parents arrived back from Arlington. Jimmy went home to take a bath and see the children. My parents hadn't been in with me long when Armedia showed up. She wanted to pray with me and see how I was doing. I was so excited to see her. My mom wanted prayer for her knee, so we gathered around her and proceeded to pray. While praying, it came forth that it was time to tell the prophesy, but I didn't know what I had said.

So, when we finished praying for my mom she started crying. She said, "When you were little, Donna, a minister came to Anderson, South Carolina. He called up the family and said one of the children was going to go through a great scrutiny. Satan was going to try to kill them, but they would come back seventy thousand times stronger. Millions would be saved and healed through these hands." Then she said, "I thought it was Lamar for the longest time. He was always going through so many trials and trying to find himself. He had a photographic memory and I thought that it was a special gift from God. Then I thought it might be Shelly. She struggled with life at first, but I knew that you and your sister were very close and you would help her make it through. But I see now that it was you, Donna. I had a calling on my life as a young woman, to sing in the choir and minister to people. Your grandmother always said that the Lord had given me a special voice with the anointing to go with it. I chose not to walk in my calling so I guess the Lord passed it down to you. Even as a young child you were very bold in your beliefs. When you got saved you told everyone about Jesus and made sure we were all saved. You even insisted that we made Shelly and Mike go to church." We hugged for the longest time and I told my parents how much I loved them.

Visiting hours were over and everyone left my side. This was the first night that I would get to be alone since I had been put in the hospital the week before. At first it felt a little strange, but I knew our Lord had not brought me this far to leave me now.

Even when we are too weak to have any faith left, he remains faithful to us and will help us, for he cannot disown us who are part of himself, and he will always carry out his promises to us (2 Tim. 2:13 LIVING).

During the time I was in the hospital and even till this day, I would try to pray without ceasing. Rejoice evermore. Pray without ceasing (1 Thess.5:16-17 KJV)

My Lord is a part of my every waking moment. He sticks closer than a brother.

A man that hath friends must shew himself friendly: and there is a friend that sticketh closer than a brother (Pro18:24 KJV)

He is my everything. That night I prayed and asked the Lord about what my mom had said. I knew that you take prophesy with a grain of salt. I knew prophesy was the deep truth of God, but it had to be confirmed in my spirit. What I heard in my spirit was that the prophesy is fulfilled thirty-three years later. Now I knew what the cloud represented that I saw in my room in CCU. I got up and reached for my tape deck so I could listen to my tape, but it wouldn't work so I blew a kiss at the camera and crawled in bed. I said my nightly prayer and fell fast asleep.

Chapter 15

SPIRITUAL ATTACK

Suddenly, it felt like millions of demons came in the room and there was such heaviness and a cold dark feeling. Even in my deep sleep it felt like they were pulling my hair and biting me. I literally felt my spirit leave my body. I was fighting with everything in me. I looked up in the corner of the room and I saw the Lord's face. He wasn't smiling like he had been the days before. He had a blank stare on his face. Then he started laughing, I said "You are laughing?"

Then I heard, "You know what to do, girl."

I got bold and I started telling those demons they had no power. I confronted them face to face. I knew the last book of the Bible, Revelation 20:10 and that the cross gave me power over them. Satan puts obstacles and circumstances in our way to get our eyes off the Lord. Right away I attacked that fear with God's Word! "You are defeated," I said, "I rebuke you in Jesus' name. Get behind me Satan. The Word says you have no power and when I plead the blood of Jesus you have to flee. You can't cross the blood line. Satan is reminded of his defeat on Calvary when our Lord shed his blood for us. How dare you even think after what I have been through that I'm going to give into you now! You are dumb for even trying." (Rev 12:11 KJV) They overcame him by the blood of the Lamb, and by the word of their testimony.

I guess he thought fear would keep me from running into the arms of my Daddy God. I had news for him! The Lord had given me a new boldness. This rose up in me from the tips of my toes. Out of my belly flowed these words "I rebuke you in Jesus' name. Satan you have to leave. You have no choice but to pull out. Your power is slipping from your hands just with my one word, Jesus! Jesus!"

Behold, I give unto you power to tread on serpents and scorpions, and over all the power of the enemy and nothing shall by any means hurt you (Luke 10:19 KJV).

Suddenly, all those little demons flew in terror right out the window with a high pitched squeal. They were very little scrawny things with pointed noses and little tiny legs. Their knees were knocking together.

Finally, I said, "You can't touch this." I lifted my arm toward the window and they were all gone. Then I started praising God again. The Lord's presence filled the room and then I saw his face again. He was smiling. I said, "Thank you Jesus for loving me." I had felt an attack like this one other time in my life, but I thought at that time it was a bad dream. I knew this was the attack of the enemy again. Satan was really mad at me. I was telling everyone about Jesus and he thought he could stop me. He wants us out of the presence of God. He knows that is where our strength comes from. He has been in God's presence and he didn't want any part of it. He thought he could get me with fear. It's time to put our finger under the devil's nose and say what the Bible says. We have power over principalities. Let's invade the Devil's territory and take back what Satan has stolen from us. Let's take back cities, states, and then America.

For God hath not given us the spirit of fear; but of power, and of love, and of a sound mind (2 Tim1:7 KJV).

I had been through so much. I was stronger in the Lord now more than ever and I knew where I stood. I was learning how powerful and real the Bible was becoming to me. I was going to praise the Lord and wait for the day that he splits the eastern sky and takes me home. I was learning how to use the Scriptures. I wrote down everything that happened and then I quickly fell back to sleep.

Suddenly, about 4:30a.m. I heard, "Code blue, 6112. Code blue, 6112." I had a sudden urgency to pray. I started praying for the person in 6112 and then the ones that had to listen to that awful machine. I prayed for the families and then everyone else in the whole hospital. I prayed till about 5:30 a.m. I felt a sense of release and knew everything was OK. I thanked God and went into the kitchen to make coffee and start my day. I was getting stronger with each passing day.

Chapter 16

THE MESSENGER

It was Friday October 23, 1999 and I had been in the hospital since the seventeenth. Maybe I would be able to go home soon. My son, Joshua had a birthday on the twenty-fifth and I would like to be out to give him a party, but I needed to take one day at a time. Soon the maid entered my room to clean my floor. This was the same maid who had cleaned my room six times prior in the CCU days before. I had told her about Jesus and even gave her a card from Bethel Temple.

She told me that I needed to go to CCU. A man that had been admitted at the same time I was, had been on a respirator and pronounced brain dead. They were going to unplug him today. She told me she wished I could be with the family.

I told her I would talk to the head nurse and see what she says. As soon as the maid left, I set out to find the nurse. She was right outside my door. I told her about the man and begged her to let me go back to the CCU.

She said that she couldn't; the monitors wouldn't pick me up down there. So I went back to my room extremely upset. Then I prayed that the Lord would send me a messenger. The word hardly came forth out of my mouth and in came a man named Brian from our church. As soon as he came in, I jumped up and said, "Praise God, you are my messenger." I told him the situation and asked him if he would go be with the family. I handed him a little bottle of anointing oil. I smiled as he left the room. Our Lord God had come through again. My prayers were getting answered immediately.

Though the day I had many visitors. I even refused breathing treatments several times because I was sharing about our Lord Jesus. One of the medical reports they wrote said, "All she wants to do is share about her healing, she is a remarkable woman." One other doctor wrote, "She went against all odds of survival; she must have someone on her side." I knew who that someone was. Maybe, now the doctors would realize who he is too. This week had to bring even the doctors to a new understanding about the power of prayer and the ultimate promises of our Lord and his Word. Everything that had happened was ordained from God.

There were many angels the Lord sent my way. I knew it wasn't by accident that I had a Baptist preacher's wife as my head nurse or by just consequence that I knew my nurse's brother in CCU from twenty-one years back. We spent all night long talking about the goodness of God and catching up on old times. He told me you can hardly be a nurse in CCU and not believe in God. He knew everything I said was the truth. He had seen so many miracles in the time he'd worked at Hendricks Hospital. Sometimes people just close their eyes and don't believe, but I don't see how he can be denied.

The Lord had sent guardian angels to be by my side, even a gray-haired man that was seen only once, who just came up and asked to pray with the family. There was a woman who gave Joni a book on God's promises she read to me over and over again. Some people would say it was just the way it worked out, but I know my Lord and I know this was all planned. It was his definite plan. He was giving me the desires of my heart. I wanted more than life itself to be used of the Lord. I had watched shows on Christian TV and seen many miracles in my life. I just wanted to be all that I could be for his glory. I knew the Word said he would guide us with his eyes, and I had prayed for the Lord many times to fill me with himself. I would be so consumed in his presence that when I walked into a room people could see Jesus—the light that only comes from his presence, the Father of Lights. I wanted to pray for people to be healed and I wanted to be filled with the anointing so strong that I couldn't stand. I want to stay in the anointing where the yoke of sickness is destroyed and problems are solved. That only comes from staying in his Word and through prayer, praise, and worship. I knew that our Lord would give us the desires of our hearts.

Delight thyself also in the LORD; and he shall give thee the desires of thine heart (Ps.37:4 KJV).

He is the same yesterday today and forever, Jesus Christ the same yesterday, and to day, and for ever (Heb. 13:8 KJV).

When he died on the cross and rose again and came into my heart the miracles he did I could do also. Verily, verily, I say unto you, he that believeth on me, the works that I do shall he do also; and greater works than these shall he do; because I go unto my Father (John 14:12 KJV).

At that moment we became one. The Lord doesn't promise us that we'll not have any problems, but he does say he will not put any more on us than we can handle and he will carry us through the hard times and the storms of life if we depend on him.

Chapter 17

WHO ARE YOU?

This had been a day of total amazement. To think that our God would answer my prayers before I even got them out of my mouth. I was learning more and more about the Lord Jesus everyday. This had been an experience like some I'd heard about, but I would never have thought our Lord would have picked a average Christian girl who hungered deeply for more of the things of God and filled her to overflowing like he'd done me. The Word says he will give you the desires of your heart; that Word was coming more real every day. I sat and pondered on the things the Lord had shown me so far and went over all the notes that I'd written. I wondered if the Lord was going to have another word for me that night and I could hardly wait for bedtime.

As I sat in my room, I suddenly got an urge for a cup of coffee, so I got up and went to see if there was any made. As I got my coffee and started back to my room, the Lord said, *Go talk to that one.*

I knew exactly who he was talking about. I was wearing my nightgown and housecoat which had wires sticking our everywhere, and I walked slowly down a long hall to the waiting area to where this woman was. There were several people in the waiting room and a woman who looked like a lady friend from church. I slowly went and sat down in the chair right beside her. She was talking to another woman. As I sat

73

there drinking my coffee her friend looked over to me and said "Who are you?" She saw me when I was coming down the hall and said I was gleaming with a glow.

I told her, "I am the woman that died yet I lived to tell about it."

They both stopped their conversation and just looked at me. As they turned toward me I noticed this wasn't the woman I thought it was. I told her I thought she was someone else from my church and I was very sorry. She looked very strangely at me, got up, and quickly walked away.

Her friend moved over by me, so I introduced myself and asked who was in the hospital? She said, "My name is Linda. I am from Cross Plains, Texas. My father-in-law is having heart surgery."

I told her to stand on Scriptures and speak life over him and he'd be OK. Then I told her about me and how the Lord had sent the healing light from heaven and healed me. We spent the next hour talking about the miracle of life and what the Lord had shown me so far.

She said, "When you were walking down the hall, I recognized the anointing that was on you." She then asked if she could tell her Pastor about me at Living Waters Ministries. She said, "When you are able, I would love for you to come and speak."

I responded, "I would love to." We hugged like we had known each other our whole lives and I went back to my room.

The nurses didn't like for me to get too far away. They were always trying to find me. They had to go to the end of the hall and look at the monitor just to know where I was. I went into my room praising God, not knowing what this would bring. Maybe this will be my first speaking engagement at a church. I knew if I was going to minister to millions this would be a start, I just had to get out of the hospital first. I decided to call my family and get ready for bed.

As I lay there thanking God for the things that had happened, I humbly bowed before him. I felt so unworthy for the gift I had received, yet I knew that the Lord must have a calling on my life or he would have taken me on to heaven to stay. God possesses all the knowledge there is, and nothing ever takes him by surprise. I put my tape in and turned off the light. Quietly I sang praises to the Lord and waited for his glory to fall. The way I had been feeling this week was extraordinary, it was so wonderful.

Worship is an attitude of the heart in which the heart bows down before God. No one else is present. There are no thoughts in your mind other than God. I didn't come with a petition. I didn't come with a request. I didn't have any needs other than to love him. I came before him because I loved him so much and I felt the need to express that love. He had healed my heart and died for me. I knew if I poured out my love, he would then pour his out upon me. I want to know him intimately so I can present and describe him to others. I wanted my love for Jesus to be so contagious that others will say, "I want to love God like she does."

The presence of God was so strong I didn't know if it could get much better. As I lay there in the dark, a light entered the room. Then again I saw the Lord's face smiling at me. I was getting accustomed to being in God's presence and I never wanted it to leave me. Then I heard, *I will never leave you nor forsake you.* I just started praising God. I was so in love with a love I had never felt in my whole life. I loved my husband and family, but this was so different. I longed for the nights I could lie and rest and see his face. I was so enthroned in my God's glory, it felt like when the light fell down from heaven and healed me. It was a feeling that I would never forget nor did I ever want to live without it again. I stayed reading the Bible and learning all that I could. I felt like there was not enough time in the day. When you are in God's presence the anointing comes, then the glory follows closely behind it.

I was learning how to stay in his presence. I would pray, then praise him, and then worship in song. By the time I'd get to worship, the anointing would fall and sometimes it was even hard to stand. That is when yokes are broken, and he will fill you with his love and glory.

Chapter 18

VISION OF A MOUNTAIN

As I lay there, I saw a vision of a great big mountain, and I was on top of it. There were people lined up all the way down, and they were just white beings. Above me there was a city of pure gold, bright and glorious; a city like I had never seen before in my whole life.

In the vision he took me to a towering mountain peak, and from there I watched that wondrous city, the holy Jerusalem, descending out of the skies from God (Rev. 21:10 LIVING).

Behind me was the lake of fire. People would come up to the top of the mountain and I would scream, "No!" But one by one, they would shoot up to heaven. Then one of the people walking up the hill fell into the lake of fire. I heard the screams and there was a smell of sulfur filling my room. Then the bright light came and I saw an image of the Lord's face, a giant tear fell and put the fire out. I knew what the Bible said, and I knew it said the lake of fire would never be put out, so I didn't understand what the Lord was trying to tell me. As I lay there, I remember saying, "Oh Lord, help me to interpret what you are trying to tell me."

Then I heard him say, *How many have you let slip through without introducing them to me?* Then he said, *Don't! You will be accountable for the ones you let slip through. How many opportunities do you let slip right by, without introducing them to your glorious God? The people are out there just waiting for you to have me as your main focus in your life. Let me fill your cup to overflowing then I will give you a bigger cup each day. The time is short. Go Now! Go Now! Go now!*

I knew I didn't want the blood of my brother on my hands, so I was determined more than ever before to share with everyone that even got close to the room. I would share not only my healing but how to accept the Lord Jesus as their Savior. I would tell them the Lord knocks; all you have to do is open the door. Ask, believe, confess, and you will be saved. So I say to you, if you hear the Lord's voice telling you to share with someone about him, you had better go. If we don't and they get in a car accident and are killed we could all be accountable. He wants us to tell everyone there is a better way of life. He is the truth and light; the Alpha, Omega; the beginning and the end. He is number one in my life.

Our Lord always speaks to us. He speaks through Bible, prayer, circumstances, and the church or other believers. He who is of God, hears God's voice. He will know his Father's voice. When God speaks to you by the Holy Spirit, you will know it is God. That is an encounter with God. In the Old Testament God spoke many times and in a variety of ways; by angels (Gen.16), visions (Gen.15), dreams (Gen.28:10-19), a gentle whisper (1 Kings 19-12), and miraculous signs (Ex. 8:20-25). When your Lord comes and speaks to you he always has a purpose for your life.

Today our Lord speaks through the Holy Spirit. Our Lord works through circumstances. I would have never chosen to walk through the valleys of sickness I have been through, but you can never have a testimony without a test. When we go through a major sickness or any other major thing in our life, most people run to God or they blame God. He is always there no matter what we are feeling. I chose to endure to the end. I know my Lord Jesus is a healing God. He came through for me and many others. We stood on him and he showed up like he always does.

Long ago, God spoke in many different ways to our fathers through the prophets, in visions, dreams, and even face to face, telling them little by little about his plans. But now in these days he has spoken to us through his Son to whom he has given everything and through whom he made the world and everything there is (Heb. 1:1-2 LIVING).

I lay there still and just humbly bowed before him. I basked in his glory and the deepness of the assignment he was calling me to. I felt he was trying to take me into a different realm. A higher level than I ever had been in before. I knew I didn't understand all that I had seen, but I knew in due time all would be explained. I had such a hunger for more of the things of God and even cried out in the darkest of night. Before this sickness, oh, how I wanted to be used for his glory. I wanted a more intimate relationship with the Father. I would beg for his glory and his anointing to fall on me. He gave me the desires of my heart through this healing. Now I have the boldness I need to do all the things the Lord has called me to do. Now I will be able to pray for the sick and see them healed. Oh, how my heart longed for that. A sickness that drives you closer to Jesus is a priceless treasure. The glory that I felt so far this week was remarkably overwhelming. The anointing was so strong it was hard for me to stand. I basked in his glory and got ready to finish writing.

Then I saw a city. It had houses on both sides of the street. I was walking down the street and knocking on doors and the people would come out of their houses and follow me. It started getting dark, and we were frantically getting people out of their homes. There was a light on both sides of us. As the crowd became bigger and bigger, we moved faster. There were demons flying toward the light that surrounded all of us but falling off at a faster rate of speed than they were coming. One by one we went to every house in the city and brought everyone into the street.

Then I saw a hill. The Lord was sitting on his throne. All the people that we had gathered were all bowing before our Lord. Praise God. It's time that we all come boldly to the throne. Our Lord is waiting for us at the right hand of the Father. He is our answer for everything in life.

Then I saw a huge house. It was shaped like an embassy and huge, like the White House. There was a very long hall. A man and woman were standing at the end of the hall. The man was a heavyset man and I remember the woman as having dark hair and she was short. People of all races and cultures were lined-up walking toward the two of them. As I lay there in amazement, I asked the Lord if it was me. I thought maybe my husband, family, and I would be in a foreign country, but he never confirmed that to me. I felt like it will be someone I knew. As the people got to the couple they kissed them on both cheeks and let them into their home. To this day I am not sure exactly what this means. The Lord will reveal it in his timing. I stopped, lay there still and quieted, and then I proceeded to start writing again.

By this time it was early Saturday morning and I hadn't been to sleep since Thursday night. The Lord gave me rest in himself. I felt like I had slept for two days.

And he said, my presence shall go with thee, and I will give thee rest (Ex. 33:14 KJV).

I had all this energy and I knew it could only come from the presence of God that I could feel so refreshed. The smell of sweet flowers entered the room and lingered throughout the morning and all day. People who visited even asked me about the sweet smell. I put up my pen and got ready for my day. When the Lord God is showing you things in the spirit you don't sleep until he is done. He always equips us with what we need as we need it.

Soon all the doctors and nurses started to arrive to take all my vital signs. I really looked forward to this part of the day. On weekends you get a different staff of nurses, some that I had not shared with yet. Joni and JoAnn arrived first. We talked about the goodness of God and I told them when I get out I wanted to go to church first thing. I told them I had really been praying that the doctors would let me out Sunday; it was my son's birthday. Soon my husband and the boys arrived. We hugged like we hadn't seen each other in years. We were all waiting to see the doctors. I loved looking at their faces. They had given up all hope of my even surviving. They would just come in shaking their heads. I loved it.

"I give God all the glory for my healing," I would say every time they would come in. Our Lord Jesus really ministered to them without their even realizing it. I planted a seed in their lives and I watered it with prayer. I know it will come up when they need it. Maybe it will cause them to call on the Lord in their time of need. The Lord is no respecter of persons. What he did for me he will do for all who come to him and ask. The Word says ask and it will be given.

Chapter 19

GOING HOME TOMORROW

Finally the doctors came in. They talked to the family and looked at my burns. They told me I was a lucky young lady. I said, "You know luck has nothing to do with it. It was all about Jesus, all about Jesus."

The doctor just smiled. He said, "Donna you are doing surprisingly well. If you continue to improve through the night you can go home tomorrow."

Yes! Yes! I was so excited. It was my youngest son's birthday; now we can have a party. I told the doctors thank you very much for taking good care of me. Even though they were still confused at what had taken place, I knew in the back of their minds they had to know our God had come through.

Finally, it seemed like I had been in the hospital a long time. So much had happened. Would the Lord still come to me in visions when I go home? Only time would tell. I never wanted to be the same as I was before. I only wanted to move forward in the things of God.

My husband and the boys left to clean the house. "Finally mom is coming home," I heard one of them say as they walked out of the room. Through all this, my oldest son Jimmy Alan had become a responsible young man. He had just turned seventeen. He would take the other two boys to school and come up to the hospital. He made sure they were all fed and the homework was done right, then he would bring them to see me. My husband Jimmy seldom left the hospital until I started getting better. He had the waiting room ministry. After I started improving, he spent his time praying for others. My middle son Chris was eleven years old and has always been the softhearted one. I had to reassure him over and over again that I was OK, and that I would not die. I told him I will live. My little son, Josh didn't really know what was going on or he just blocked it out. It was too painful for him to think about. I told my family that I loved them more than life itself. We had become so much closer than we had ever been before. I thought I couldn't ever love them more than I did, but when you go through something like this it changes everything.

Joni and Billy's children were really upset too, especially Daniel. He was sixteen and he knew of my pain. He had such faith. He knew our Lord was going to heal me before anyone else. He was not going to stop praying until he did. The whole family stood firm on what the Word says. Tiffany was the middle little girl; she would have stayed up there with me all the time if they had let her. Then the youngest son Brandon—I think he knew more of what was going on than Josh did. His little eyes would be puffy from all his crying, but the Lord changed the sorrow into rejoicing. Praise God! Joni had been with me the whole time waiting on me hand and foot. Our whole family loved like never before. With JoAnn and Junior staying by my side, I am blessed to have a family that loves the Lord. My family is there to teach me how to be all that I can be in Christ Jesus.

My parents acquired a new relationship with the Lord Jesus. My sister started asking questions about Christ and living a saved life. My brother being a Baptist, starting searching the Scripture on what the Bible said about healing. One brother began to pray for the first time in his life, and this changed everyone. All of us have become one happy family.

I never felt so much love around me before. I knew the Lord was letting me taste his love and he was doing it through the people I love more than anything. I never let a day go by that I didn't tell my family and friends how much I loved them, now that I knew what unconditional love was. They loved me no matter what. When God invites you to join him and you face a crisis of belief, what you do next tells what you believe about God. Your actions really do speak louder than words. My family's actions showed where their hearts were.

When the Lord speaks to you, revealing what he is about to do, that revelation is your invitation to adjust your life to him. We can't continue life as usual or stay where we are and go with God at the same time. This is true all through the Scripture. When we decide to give all to the Lord and follow him, enormous changes and adjustments have to be made! After all the Lord had done for me, I wanted to give him all of me. I had a burning desire to be guided by his eyes. Nothing else seemed to matter. It didn't matter if everything was picked up and perfect. All that mattered was I was healed, walking in my Fathers foot steps, and learning to be just like him. I am learning to be a better Christian and a better mom. My family is everything to me.

Now I know what is truly important in life and it's not hurrying to get places. That is Satan's greatest offence. He gets us so busy we forget our family and our God. We are so busy with the things in life, we forget why we are living. He doesn't want us reading the Bible. That is God's love letter to us and it has all the answers to life in it; we just have to find them. Satan wants to keep them hidden. This experience sure did open my eyes. Never again do I want to be the same busy person I was unless I am doing the works of my Father. I want the Lord to keep me in his will. That way I don't get in his way. He will mold me and make me. I will be all he wants me to be.

Soon it was lunch time. I was so hungry I felt like I had not eaten in a long time. Now I could have some real food. Joni and Billy brought me a hamburger and it tasted better than I had ever remembered it tasting before. I had a lot of people come from the church to see me. I told everyone that I would get to go home tomorrow. I could hardly wait. It would take me forever to get all my stuff picked up in the room so I started boxing everything up early. This day seemed to never end. The clock seemed to be stopped. The nurses hustled in and out trying to get all my tests done and my breathing treatments finished. Finally, it was getting dark and everyone went home. I was so tired from all the work of trying to get ready to go home. I decided to lie down early. It was about 9:30 p.m. I called my family and told them I loved them, I said a prayer, and before I went to sleep. I prayed, "Lord, why?"

He responded. *Satan was trying to kill you. I allowed it to happen to give you holy boldness and to lift you up to a new spiritual realm where you are going to have to be, to do the mighty miracles that I am going to do through your hands.*

What an awesome God we have. I wrote down what I heard, praised God, and fell fast to sleep.

TODAY IS THE DAY

I woke up with a sweet smell of God's presence and I started praising God. There was still such a peace in the room. It was Sunday, October 25. This is the day I get to go home. I wanted just to dance. I was extremely happy.

Then the maid came in and told me that I needed to go pray for the man across the hall. He was going to have heart bypass surgery done. He had not been out of bed or taken a bath for days. She said, "Donna he has given up. Would you go talk to him?"

"Sure I will," and then I told her, "I will be going home today, so I will go now." I asked the Lord to give me favor and I went out of my room and walked up to his door.

There was a sign on the door that read "No Visitors," but I knew it was life or death so I went in. There he was a little tiny, skinny man in the bed. He looked almost dead. I said, "Hi, my name is Donna. I'm in the room across the hall." Then I told him how the Lord had healed me. As I started talking, he sat up to listen. I helped him up in the bed then I told him about the lights of heaven and the peace beyond understanding. He was captivated by my every word. His wife just stared at me like I was from another planet. I asked them if they had ever received Jesus Christ as their savior.

They responded by saying, "Yes a long time ago."

Then I looked right at him and I said, "The Lord loves you and he wants you to get out of this bed, take a bath, and get prayed up for your surgery. He is no respecter of persons and if he can heal me like he did I know he will heal you." I asked if I could pray for them, and said a short prayer, and we hugged bye. I told him, "Don't forget, I will be praying for you and you can pray for me." Then I left the room.

Several minutes went by. I went back to my room to get all my belongings together to go home. Suddenly the maid came running in to see me. She said, "Look Donna, look."

I came back into the hallway to see the little man that I had spoken to earlier that day. He had taken a bath and was walking down the hall, smiling from ear to ear. Our Lord is so worthy of all our praise. I told him bye and I had a peace in my spirit. I knew somehow he was going to be OK.

The doctor would be here soon, so I hurried back to my room. I called my church and told them if I get out early enough, I would be there. I kept asking the nurses when the doctor was going to arrive. They kept saying it would be soon. I was anxious to get released out of the hospital. I just wanted to be home in my own bed and with my family. I really wanted a bath but they wouldn't let me take the monitors off. Even though I had met a lot of friends since I had been in the hospital, I was ready to go home. Jimmy arrived to pick me up I started loading up all my flowers, cards, and gifts. Finally, it was only minutes away from my dream of being able to go home. I had been through so much and I was so thankful that the Lord healed me. I didn't know how the Lord was going to use this sickness, but I knew what Satan meant for evil, our Lord always turns around for his glory.

It was about 2:30 in the afternoon. Our church had already started and was over. The doctor still hadn't arrived. The nurses tried to keep me occupied, but I was impatient. Then the door opened and it was my doctor. He said they were very pleased with my recovery. He told me I would be on eight pills a day the rest of my life. I just sat there and listened to every word he said, but I knew deep down inside they would be surprised again. I was not going to be on that much medicine the rest of my life. Anytime the Lord heals you he always finishes his work, totally not partially. So I knew soon I would be off of it all. They told me that one of the diet products that I had been taking had caused this entire problem with my heart. Then he proceeded to tell me about another patient of his, a woman who was admitted into the other hospital across town the very night that I was put in. She had been on the same product that I had taken and her heart did the same thing as mine did. She, too, had recently quit taking the product when her heart started acting up. "She did not do as well as you." Then he sadly sighed.

He just looked at me and I said, "Doctor, you know why. It's my Lord. He is the one that healed me. If it wasn't for my faith in God, I probably wouldn't be here either. I know the Greater Physician."

The doctor looked puzzled. Then he said, "Don't take those diet pills any more. OK? You really gave me a scare. You are free to go as soon as the nurses get your papers done." He turned and walked out of the room.

Jimmy said, "Are you ready to get dressed?"

I said, "I just want to take a shower before we go." I started taking off all those wires and getting ready to get in and the alarms went off. That awful sound! Even though I was getting to go home, that noise still made my skin crawl.

That got the nurses attention. They ran in the room to find my husband standing outside of the bathroom door. "She really wanted a shower. The doctor told her we could go home as soon as you get the papers ready."

The water was warm against my skin. The burns had totally healed which was a miracle in itself. I took my time in the shower and just thanked God for allowing me to walk through this and come out on top. I was a survivor.

Psalm 136 is an exhortation to give thanks to God for particular mercies.

O give thanks unto the LORD; for he is good: for his mercy endureth for ever. O give thanks unto the God of gods: for his mercy endureth for ever. O give thanks to the Lord of lords: for his mercy endureth for ever. To him who alone doeth great wonders: for his mercy endureth for ever. To him that by wisdom made the heavens: for his mercy endureth for ever. To him that stretched out the earth above the waters: for his mercy endureth for ever. To him that made great lights: for his mercy endureth for ever. (Ps. 136:1-7 KJV).

I had been miraculously, instantly healed.

Jimmy came to the door and told me to hurry. "The nurses are in here waiting on you."

I said OK and got out and dried off. It felt really strange putting on my clothes. It seemed like I had been in my nightgown forever. A total of eight days I had been in this hospital. As I signed the release papers I felt sad. It seemed like all the emotions of all week were coming down on me all at once. They were welling up in my spirit, both happiness and sadness. I really didn't know what to feel.

I knew when I went home I wouldn't have the people to minister to. I had not seen daylight all week, except when I looked out the third floor window. I wrote a thank you note and told the nurse I would like to go by CCU on my way out. She put me into my wheelchair and out of the door we went. We quickly went down the hall and I told all the nurses bye, then into the elevator. Finally we were back in CCU. I quickly said a silent prayer for everyone in there and I gave the nurse on duty my note. They pushed me by, and I took one last look at my old room and left. Jimmy had gone to get the car. The nurses asked me to keep in touch. The car arrived and I got in.

REALITY SETS IN

I sat there and looked up at the sky. It was so blue; the clouds were fluffy white. There were streaks of pink all in the sky. I never remember seeing the sky so beautiful. Everything around me looked greener and brighter. I felt like I was seeing everything for the first time in my life. It must have been like that for the blind man in the Bible when he was brought to Jesus and the Lord healed him. He saw every man clearly. It must have been overwhelming with so much joy. It was so hard to keep it to himself, but the Lord said to go and tell no one. The Lord said to me, *Go and share the testimony of what I have done for you,* and that is what I intended to do—go into all the earth and share the good works of the Lord. We finally arrived at the house and our boys were in the yard playing soccer. They came running to me and hugged me like I had been away for a very long time. What a journey I had been on and I knew it had just begun. It was hard to hold back the tears of joy and the relief I felt. Jimmy helped me out of the car and I went into the house. It was sparkling clean. My family had done a great job keeping it up.

I asked for my tape and told Jimmy I wanted to go lie down. My spirit was still soaring but my flesh was weak. As soon as I lay down on the bed, I started to cry. I cried and cried. I think I finally realized how close to death I was, and then it dawned on me that I had actually died.

I had never cried so hard in my whole life. Jimmy came running in to check on me and held me for a long time, and we cried together. I had been so strong through these eight days. I was so focused on what the Bible said and how the Lord was going to come through and heal me. I didn't show much emotion. I had to be strong for everyone around me. Now I was home and my emotions came rolling in like an ocean wave.

My boys stood at the door just watching me cry. I told them to come in, I hugged them, and said I would be OK. "I really do love you boys, do you know that?" All three of them nodded their heads yes and they went outside to finish their game. After a few minutes I was fine. The joy came and I was so overwhelmed. My Lord actually loved me so much that he healed me. Wow, I realized.

This sickness is not unto death, but for the glory of God that the Son of God may be glorified through it (John 11:4 KJV). Finally the blinders were off of my eyes. I began to see what God had in mind for my circumstance. Through this sickness and this healing God was glorified in the eyes of his people. Because of this healing, many people sensed a fresh call to prayer. They personally began to experience a new presence of truth—and truth as a person. People that never knew the power of prayer before started to pray.

God did bring glory to himself through this sickness. Do you see what happened? We faced a trying situation. We could have looked back at God from the middle of the situation and gotten a much distorted understanding of God, but instead, we went to him. We sought out his perspective on the situation. The Holy Spirit took the Word of God and revealed to us God's perspective on the end result of that circumstance. We believed God and adjusted our lives to him. We talked like I had already been healed before it even came to pass. We then went through the circumstance looking for ways that his purpose would be accomplished and would bring him glory. So when the answer to prayer came, I knew immediately that my job was to declare the wonderful works of the Lord to his people. In the process I came to know God in a new way because of the compassion. I know that the Lord is going to use me, I don't know how yet, but I will.

Joni and JoAnn came over to check on me. They wanted to know if I had taken all my medicine. I was on so much it was hard to remember when to take it. So we wrote it down and put it on the refrigerator. I had a tiring day. Just getting out of the hospital, and getting so emotional took all the strength I had left. I talked to them for a few minutes; then I went to bed.

I lay there in the dark praising God for allowing me to walk through this dark place in my life. I knew what Satan meant for destruction, God would turn around for his glory. I looked forward to every passing moment. As I lay there, I felt the presence of God. I had wondered if it would be the same when I came home. The Lord gave me this Scripture: "Whither shall I go from thy spirit? Or whither shall I flee from thy presence? If I ascend up into heaven, thou art there: if I make my bed in hell, behold, thou art there. If I take the wings of the morning, and dwell in the uttermost parts of the sea; Even there shall thy hand lead me, and thy right hand shall hold me (Ps. 139:7-10 KJV)

Then I saw the bright light and the glory of his love. Every time I shut my eyes I saw bright lights. I knew by this that my Lord was with me; I felt him.

I will never leave you or forsake you. There shall not any man be able to stand before thee all the days of thy life: as I was with Moses, so I will be with thee: I will not fail thee, nor forsake thee (Josh. 1:5 KJV).

I fell fast asleep. Soon it was morning. I heard the children moving around in the other room. Jimmy had taken a two week vacation from work, so he was getting the boys ready for school. It must have been a relief to Jimmy Alan not having to do it. All three of my boys came in hugged me and told me they loved me. Then my oldest said, "Mom I'm sure glad you are OK. I love you."

"I love you too Jimmy Alan," I said. "I will see you when you get home."

The phone starting ringing, everyone was calling to see how my morning was going. I got out of bed and made my coffee. Jimmy's sister, Linda wanted to come over and see me. All the people from the church wanted to bring us food. Everyone wanted to do everything for me. I had people calling wanting to pick up my kids and even clean my house. Anything I needed was at my fingertips. But instead of being excited, I felt helpless. I had always been one to do everything myself. I never had to depend on anyone for anything. If it needed fixing, I just fixed it. I had helped work on our cars and even done plumbing. I picked up the kids, cleaned the house, worked, and made dinner. I was always the one to take my boys to soccer practice on two different sides of town. I went to all the school functions; I had never been away from my family one time until this happened. I'd never depended on others for anything. I thought I was supermom.

Now reality was hitting me like a ton of bricks. I might have to depend on others to help me. I wasn't able to do all the things I normally did. I needed time to get my strength back. I just didn't want anyone to know I might need help, except for my family of course. They knew what I was capable of doing and it wasn't much. They tried to help in a way so I wouldn't feel helpless. When people would call wanting to come over, I would tell them I was fine. Then I would break down in tears. It was a hard adjustment for me. I was lying in bed praying and the Lord said, *Donna, if you don't let them help, you rob them of their blessing.*

I told Jimmy what I had heard. He said, "Donna, the Lord has healed you and given you a story to tell. Everyone wants to know what it was like being so close to God. They want to be in God's presence and they think they can get that from talking to you."

"But you know, Jimmy, it has nothing to do with me. It's all about Jesus. It's all about him," I said.

"He wants you to share your testimony, but you can't if you close out the ones who help you."

"I don't want anyone to lose their blessings because of me, so I will let people help."

Jimmy said, "OK babe, whatever you think, but you know it will be adjustment."

I said, "You will have to help me change my way of thinking." I think the Lord was teaching me an important lesson. God's number one interest in the world is for them to come to know him. The only way people will know what God is like is when they see him work. They knew this healing was beyond what people could do because he demonstrated his nature, his strength, his provision, and his kindness to his people and to a watching world through me. I was going to be his vessel. He had chosen me. I so wanted to be used for his glory. I·hungered for more of God and now it was coming to pass.

Linda arrived almost at lunch time. We talked a long time on the couch. She gave me the book *Angels* by Billy Graham and a tape with one of my nieces singing a song that she had made at church. I knew that it would be good and I couldn't wait to hear it. She asked if I felt like going out to lunch at Furrs Cafeteria. I was still really tired, but I knew I could do all things through Christ that strengthens me. So I got ready and we went to eat. As we came home, the phone was ringing. My answering machine was full. Everyone you could think of had called.

I ran in and grabbed the phone. It was my mom and dad. They would be back down this weekend and if I needed them before that I was to call. Mom said, "Donna, the Lord has giving me a poem for you. When I finish it, I will call you."

I couldn't imagine what it would be about. My mom and dad had not always been close to the Lord, I prayed for them all the time. Now they were both praying and spending time in the Word. My dad had been saved about five years ago. He had started going to church soon after that. The doctors had told him he had cancer and was going to have surgery. Through this awful experience my dad got healed and saved. Again, what Satan meant for destruction, the Lord turned around for his glory. The Lord was teaching us all to depend on him for our needs.

My mom was saved when she was a child. She would sing in the choir and do specials she even wrote some songs. But growing up, I don't remember going to church much. I felt the Lord was bringing the whole family to a new understanding of him. Joni and JoAnn had always loved the Lord but this experience brought them to a new level, one were we all wanted to be but couldn't ever seem to reach in our own strength, a new realm.

After dinner Linda went home, so I decided to go and lie down. I just wanted to thank God for everything. My boys came home from school, and I helped Joshua with his homework. I felt like everything was getting back to normal. But I had been changed forever. I would never be the same mom again. The things that used to seem important to me were no longer important. My God and my family were number one just like they should have always been.

Joni, Billy, and the kids came by to see me. After being with them eight days straight, I felt lost when they didn't stay long. But they had let everything go too. We had to get back into life and come back into reality. I hugged them like I had not seen them in forever. We talked and then they left.

After supper we took our baths and it was time for bed again. Jimmy and I talked about the things of God. There was so much they didn't talk about at the Baptist church he was going to. He asked, "Donna, what does the Bible say about healing?"

I started explaining about the healing and the Holy Spirit. I told him about the anointing that breaks every yoke. I said "Jimmy, the anointing of God is transferable. God is not limited in ways that he heals. He uses the hands of men to transfer the anointing and can use any article he desires that will achieve the end result. In Acts 19:11-12 the Word says, "And God was performing extraordinary miracles by the hands of Paul, so that handkerchiefs or aprons were even carried from his body to the sick, and the diseases left them, and the evil spirits went out." So you see, that explains why I believe in the prayer cloths. Our God can do anything. He spoke our whole universe into place with one word. It's his good pleasure to heal, deliver, and set our feet on solid ground. He loves us more than we could ever know. The Holy Spirit was sent to us to be our guide and comfort when our Lord went into heaven."

The Lord always wants to meet us on the level of faith we have; then we grow with his mighty guidance. He asked me about speaking in tongues. I told him that was another gift that our Father wants us to receive. I called it my heavenly language. "It's between me and God. When I speak in tongues, the spirit prays what I need most in my life—not what I feel or think I need but what the Lord knows I need. I will look the Scriptures up tomorrow for you."

He knew since I had been healed, he could never go back to his church and he had too many questions. "Why don't they teach that part of the Bible?" he asked.

I really didn't know all the answers but I believed the Bible from Genesis to Revelation. The Bible has a spiritual side and a literal side. I didn't know if he would go to church with me or not, but I was planning to go Wednesday. I had been praying for him to go with me. But I wasn't going to beg him anymore. As long as he was going, that was all that was important. I loved my husband's Baptist pastor. He is a special man of God and I attended that church for a long time. He checked on me every day I was in the hospital and spent a lot of time ministering to Jimmy. He even told his congregation about my healing. The deeper my walk became with the Lord, the more I searched the Scriptures. I felt in my spirit there was so much more and no one wanted to talk about it.

My niece had shared previously a little about her church with me and told me about all the miracles that were happening. She said, "They have a wonderful children's program. You need to visit."

When I started going I found all that I was searching for at this non-denominational church. All my questions were being answered by every sermon. Every time Pastor Frank spoke, it answered questions I had about what I was going through. I would find the Scripture and pray about it then Pastor would preach on it. One by one I knew I was where I was supposed to be and doing all I was called to. Our God is so good. Now I have been going to BTCC for fourteen years.

Chapter 22

DANCING IN THE
SPIRIT

It was Tuesday morning. The children's laughter brought joy to my heart. I paid attention to everything more clearly. My new day was about to begin. I stayed in bed for a while just lying in the presence of God and praising him. I would sing until the glory would fall. I love him more that anything in my life. We have an intimate relationship. My Father God, My Daddy God is a healer. He loves me so much. Wow, he is wonderful. I continued to sing, "Oh how he loves you and me, Oh how he loves you and me. He gave his life. What more could he give? Oh how he loves you. Oh how he loves me. Oh how he loves you and me."

It was soon time to get up. Jimmy had picked up the house. I was so much in love with my husband and my family. Then the phone rang. It was the church. They wanted to send Barry over to see if I needed any help with my book. He is our assistant pastor. Karen and Fern, who were the pastor's receptionist and secretary, were coming too. I had been writing every chance I had.

Soon they were at the door. I let them in and started sharing again about the goodness of our Lord. They still couldn't believe the progress I was making. We talked for a short time at the kitchen table. I excused myself and I got up to turn my tape over. This one song really stood out in my spirit. When it came on my spirit felt like it left my body and went into the living room. I got up and I started dancing. I felt like I was dancing with the Holy Spirit. I had never been one for dancing but this was different. Around and around in the living room we went. It was so awesome. I felt like I was floating. I was in my own little world. It didn't matter who was watching, I was just dancing. I knew somehow this song would be used in my ministry.

With everything I had been through, this again was something new to me. So many extraordinary things had happened. I felt like every day was a new adventure. The Lord was teaching me daily about himself. Oh, how I had limited God. I never knew he was so real before. He is truly alive. Wow! He does stick closer than a brother. He is one you can walk with and talk with. He talks to me through his Word. I had just begun my walk with the true side of our living Lord.

The look on Barry, Karen, and Fern's faces was surprise. But the anointing on the room was so strong, I new they had to fill it. Sometimes, I'd just get taken away to heaven. This was closeness with the heavenly father that I never wanted to lose. I was so tuned into everything I was to do and when I was do it. We shared a little about my book and they helped me find some Scriptures.

It was getting late into the day, so they decided to leave. I thanked them for the help and walked them to the car. The phone had been ringing all day and I had a lot of phone calls to return after they left. For the next few days I rested and let my family help me with all that was needed.

Sonya Madison had come over to see me. We were very close friends. She led worship at Bethel Temple. I knew when I was better we would be leading together and I couldn't wait. If our Lord wanted me to be a worship leader, he would have to teach me and anoint me as one. The Lord God never calls you to that which he doesn't equip you. I knew he had already called me because of the things he showed me in the hospital. Now it was up to him to make me what he wanted me to be. I was willing and able to do all.

We talked about how the Lord had healed me and I shared all the things I had seen. She wanted to see all the papers that I had written in the hospital. She said, "It just seems so unreal."

We shared what the Lord had done and the glory filled the whole house. She was so excited, no matter how many times she heard me share, it still wasn't enough and I loved telling her. My God had given me an awesome gift and I wanted everyone to be a part of it. Sonya's children would be out of school soon, so she had to leave to pick them up. The evening seemed to be approaching quickly. Since I had been home, the days were short and sweet. Every day that passed I seemed to get more strength.

It was Wednesday, October 28, 1998. I had been out of the hospital three days. I couldn't wait for 7:00 p.m. to arrive. I had already told Jimmy I wanted to go to church. He seemed concerned about my going but let me go anyway, and Jimmy Alan drove me. The doctors said I couldn't drive for six months.

Sonya was leading worship as I watched the expressions on her face. The music sounded different, more beautiful than I had ever heard before. Everyone was as happy to see me as I was to see them. They had been praying all week. I thanked them all and told them our Lord God had heard all the prayers and had come through and totally healed me. I knew Pastor Frank would let me share the whole testimony in the future. The church service was over at 8:00 p.m. and we started home.

Chapter 23

MOM'S POEM

The next few days seemed to rush by. I couldn't wait for Friday. My mom and dad were coming into town. I was really excited to hear the poem my mom had written. Since this had happened, I was learning more and more about my parents, even things I had never thought about. This was the spiritual side I had dreamed and wished for, not only for my parents, but for the whole family. I had experienced the glory of having the Lord Jesus not only as a friend, but as a Savior and a Redeemer. Everything I could ever want or need, I found in the Word of God. I was so glad to share all I had learned. This was opening my parents' understanding and putting a new light on the way I felt and looked at things.

Finally, they arrived. The first thing my mom did was bring out her poem that the Lord had given her for me. She told me she wrote a lot when she was younger. That was another part of my mom I never knew. I knew she had a voice like an angel but I didn't know she could write. I thanked God every day for allowing this to happen to me. I had received so much more than just a healing. This brought my parents to a new level with him and was worth it all. My mom said, "Here is the poem the Lord actually gave to me when I was praying. That's the way I used to get all my poems and songs."

"That's great mom," I said. "I can't wait to hear it." She handed it to me and I started to read.

Mom's Poems to Me

He's such a vision of delight,
Who came before me in the night.
There were such wonders to behold,
With all the lights of gleaming gold.
He brought me back to live again,
This one we know as Son of Man.

Each time I closed my eyes in death,
The paddles touching on my chest,
For many times it seemed as though
The Lord was ready for me to go.

With one touch of his mighty hand
He said not now this son of man.
He placed his hand upon my heart and
I could feel the beating start.

When there was nothing else that man could do,
I knew our Lord had brought me through.
Oh, what praise we felt that night
As the angles danced in sight.
This room is filled with heavenly light,
The Lord our God is here tonight.

"Praise God! Now your heart is brand new just like he promised me he would do in Ezekiel 36:26. That was so beautiful, mom. I love it," I said.

"The Lord also gave me a few more do you want to hear them? This one he gave me as dad and I drove down here. I sang it to him as I wrote. The name of it is *My Guardian Angel.*

Mom's Poem

MY GUARDIAN ANGEL

Verse: Our Father teaches us to pray,
         He guides us through each passing day.
         If you believe then you will see,
         How much my savior means to me.

Chorus: He's my guardian angel; He watches over me.
        He's my guardian angel; He sees the things I cannot see.
        He always hears me when I pray and chases all my fears
        away.
        He's my guardian angel, He watches over me.

Verse: I close my eyes to sleep at night,
         The troubles stirring up inside.
         I know it's time for me to pray,
         This helps through another day.

Chorus: He's my guardian angel; He watches over me.
        He's my guardian angel; He sees the things I cannot see.
        He always hears me when I pray and chases all my fears
        away.
        He's my guardian angel; He watches over me.

Verse: He calms the waves of a stormy sea,
         His arms outstretched to comfort me,
         He knows our needs, we should not fear,
         Our Lord is with us everywhere.

Chorus: He's my guardian angel; He watches over me.
        He's my guardian angel; He sees the things I cannot see.
        He always hears me when I pray and chases all my fears
        away.
        He's my guardian angel; He watches over me.

Then my dad said, "She wrote one more about South Carolina when she was young and when you and Mike and Shelly were little. Do you feel like hearing it to?"
I said, "Sure."
My mom started to read.

CAROLINA

Verse: Way back in Carolina, when I was just a child,
My mother played the organ, my father danced and
smiled.
They loved the old time music; it gave them so much joy.
Through I was only seven; I stood and praised the Lord.
My sisters always helped me; they held me on their knee,
And I can still remember how much this meant to me.

Chorus: I still hear the laughter, the tapping on the floor,
The music from the organ will be here evermore.
Yes, I still hear the laughter, the tapping on the floor,
The music from the organ will be here evermore.

Verse: Our family came to visit, on Sunday I recall.
Each one would bring a dish or two, with food that pleased
them all.
We all held hands and said a prayer before the meal began,
To thank Him for these things we have, our Lord, our food,
our friends.

Chorus: I still hear the laughter, the tapping on the floor,
The music from the organ will be here evermore.
Yes, I still hear the laughter, the tapping on the floor,
The music from the organ will be here evermore.

Verse: My children still remember and these memories they will
keep.
Their heads would rest upon my chest while I rocked them
off to sleep.
They loved the gospel music and others that I knew,
While I thought of Carolina, and mom and daddy too.

Chorus: I still hear the laughter, the tapping on the floor,
The music from the organ will be here evermore.
Yes, I still hear the laughter, the tapping on the floor,
The music from the organ will be here evermore.

We had a great weekend. This made us all so close, and I learned a lot more about my mom's side of the family that I didn't know.

Sunday came around and we all got up and started getting ready for church. We left the house about 10:30 in the morning. I was not going to say anything to Jimmy about going with me but somehow I felt he would. When the Lord healed me, Jimmy's eyes were opened to all that we believed in. He could no longer question healing because he had seen it happen to me. This built his faith and he realized there was so much more. I knew he would hunger for the deeper things of God. We arrived at the church, pulled in, and here came Jimmy. I was so excited to see him at our church. He had experienced firsthand how much the church loved me and our family. He had hands laid on him so many times when I was in the hospital; I knew he would never be able to return to his church. They may believe in healing they just don't express it in the same way.

He told me that there was just so much love; he had to come and be a part. "I knew by what the Lord had shown you, Donna that your calling was at Bethel Temple and I had a strong conviction that I needed to be where the family attended. If you and the boys like it at Bethel Temple Christian Center, I guess I can be happy here too."

Finally our dream had come true. The boys couldn't believe their eyes and when they saw their dad; they ran up and hugged him.

This reminded me of a vision I wrote down when I was in the hospital. I asked the Lord, "What about Jimmy?" The Lord showed me a man in a suit. It was Jimmy. Then he showed me the boys all running up to him and jumping up toward his arms. I never knew why that vision was given to me, but now I know. He was coming home into what the Lord wanted for him also. We were at church as a family like the Lord had planned for us to be.

Tomorrow, Jimmy will have to return to work and I wondered what it would feel like being alone. I knew my Lord would always be with me, but I had become accustomed to having Jimmy around.

My parents had to return home after church. So after they left, I spent the rest of the day in the presence of God praising him. I love him so much. I just wanted to be everything he wanted. I didn't want one day to go by that I wasn't in his perfect will. I had learned that you only receive God's perfect will by staying in communication with him.

Chapter 24

MY FIRST SPEAKING ENGAGEMENT

Through the next few weeks and months my strength returned. Every day that passed, I spent in prayer with our Lord. He guided my every waking moment.

I was in church almost every service. By November 28, 1998, I had already helped Sonya with my very first song service and spoke at our church. I was walking toward the calling the Lord had for me. A pastor called me from Cross Plains, Texas and wanted me to come speak at her church. Sometimes as Christians we have to take the first step, and then the Lord carries us. The Lord was guiding me with his eyes. I was just listening to my spirit and following his lead.

Every day was a new experience. Before I was sick, I hungered for the deeper things of God and asked to know him more personally, and now he was giving me the desires of my heart. I had heard of people dying and going into the lights of heaven before, and I was always curious to hear the whole story. Now the Lord allowed me to be lifted up into that heavenly realm where Jesus sits at the right hand of the Father and where the love is more apparent than I had ever known before. This love is more than a human could ever experience in a whole lifetime, even more than a mother for a new born baby. Oh what love! I felt so blessed just to receive one glimpse of this glory, just to have one drop of that love and be able to see the lights of the golden city. And oh, the peace beyond understanding is so wonderful. And he loves us all that much. Wow! Our Lord is no respecter of persons. What he did for me he will do for all. The other side of life he showed me, and he will show all who believe; if they only ask him into their lives they will never be the same. There are only two ways to go, heaven or hell. Don't wait till it's too late; chose heaven; chose Jesus. He is the way, the truth, and the light. There is only one way to the Father and it's through Jesus, that's what the Bible says.

Every time I went to the doctor, he was amazed at the progress I was making. I was later told that I was the talk of my doctor's hunting trip. Through this I know my doctors had changed their thinking on miracles. My family doctor searched the medical records again and again, still finding no medical reason I should be alive and doing so well. Now months later, he calls me a miracle child and tells me I have guardian angels all around me. I planted that seed about our Lord Jesus and now he is asking questions.

A few days before I left to speak at Cross Plains, everything started going wrong. Satan was so mad at me and now I was doing just what he feared. I was sharing with the world about the healing I had received and the fight I had won through Jesus against him and his little demons. The night before it was time for me to go to Cross Plains, my nephew Dwight (Joni's brother) and his wife, came over to see me. They had been praying for me and the Lord had given them the Scripture, Luke 4:16-24. I thanked them and quickly went to read it. He told me that a prophet is not accepted in his own country. I knew the Lord was about to do something special.

That Sunday morning we got up and started toward Cross Plains. I prayed the whole way there that the words that came out of my mouth would be ordained of God. I wanted it to be a testimony for him and the people to see the true light of God that was shining in me. When we arrived, I introduced myself and my husband and I went into the pastor's study to pray. Then I heard the music. I came out of the office and saw several people walking around with banners and flags, singing and praying. They were walking around the whole church even outside.

I entered the sanctuary and started singing and worshiping the Lord. You could feel the excitement in air. Linda had shared a little about me and the hospital with them. The pastor introduced me and I came up front to speak. At first I was so scared I kept saying to myself that fear is not of God and I would not give in to Satan's tricks. I knew the Lord had called me to this and he was going to have to be the one to make it come to pass through me. I had never been one to stand up in front of a lot of people before but as I prayed, my new boldness that our Lord had given me came forth. I knew this would be the first of many speaking engagements. I knew in my heart I had to tell all the Lord had done for me. Then I prayed for the sick. All who came received something from God. I told everyone it had nothing to do with me. It was all about Jesus; all about Jesus. The service was great. They took up an offering for me and I was so blessed. I would have shared with them for nothing. The Lord always takes care of his own.

Chapter 25

ALBANY CHURCH

The months passed quickly and soon it was Christmas. I just kept writing in my book every chance I had and I knew it would be finished in God's timing, not mine. Soon the pastor from Albany, Texas had called and asked me to come and share what God had done. I prayed about it first, then I felt in my spirit it was time, so agreed to go. I was looking forward to another chance to minister and pray for the sick.

This was beginning of a new year and what a way to start it out. I looked forward to every phone call. I had still been telling everyone about my healing, even the telemarketer. The pastors that had called me so far had heard about my healing and wanted the whole story. It was so great that I didn't have to look for places to speak. The doors just opened up. The Lord says he will open the doors and that our steps are ordered by him. I couldn't wait to see what the Lord had in store for my life.

Soon it was time to go to Albany to speak. About the time we were going to leave the house, a really bad storm moved through town. The weather looked awful. I knew Satan didn't want me to speak in Albany because of all the battles that had gone on this week. I had been pleading the blood and telling him to get behind me. I was prayed up and I knew no matter what Satan tried to pull, I had to speak. I felt in my spirit the same excitement as I did in the hospital. I knew it was God's will for me to go, and I wasn't going to let anything stop me. My husband and I prayed and left for Albany.

As soon as we arrived, Brother Don met me at the door and told me he tried to call me; the whole town was out of electricity. The church had several people in it already. I stopped and prayed to myself, *Lord I know it's your will for me to speak. Oh Father, what shall I do?* Then it was like I knew in my spirit the meeting must go on, so I asked Brother Don, "Do you think we can find some candles, oil lamps and flashlights?"

He responded by saying, "Yes."

I told him the Lord was already here and in control of this situation, and he wanted me to speak. I was not going to let Satan win. He is a defeated foe.

I met people at the door and asked them to go bring what they had from their cars and houses. I felt like a little girl getting ready for my first camping trip. I was so excited. The church quickly filled up with people.

We started our service by candle light. The music was so anointed even though we were singing a cappella. The Lord had shown up and was walking in our midst. My boys all moved to the third row from the front where they could hear since there was no PA system.

Soon it was my turn. I shared my testimony and even felt led, so I sang a couple of songs. I said, "Let there be light," and all the lights came on. I thanked the Lord and said, "Perfect timing" as everyone was clapping. I said, "You know the Lord is in this place and he wants to meet your every need, no matter how big or how small. Our Jesus cares about all we care about. He is no respecter of persons. What Jesus has done for me, he will do for all who come boldly to the throne. This is what Word of God says." Then I said, "If anyone would like me to pray for them, please come forward."

I asked Brother Don to come forward and help. The isles were filling up with people. I had never prayed for so many people in my whole life. The power of God was so strong it was really hard to stand up. I would anoint my hands with oil and before I even got to pray for a lot of them, they were falling under the power of God. I moved my arm around to get the holy oil and the whole first three rows of people went down. This power is greater than any locomotive. Although we cannot see it, we can feel it. The tangible presence of anointing of God is available to every believer. The kind of anointing that we had experienced came from heaven, from Christ the anointed one.

We had one woman I prayed for who had hurt her ankle, and it was swelling in her boot. They asked me to pray for her again. I knew Satan was trying to stop the great work the Lord was doing. So I laid my hands on her ankle and told Satan that he was a liar and he was not going to steal her healing. Immediately her ankle went down like a deflated balloon. She took off her boot and started running around the room. Our Lord had come through and totally, instantly healed her. Everyone started dancing and praising God. We were all in awe of his glory. We had people lying everywhere.

Then the pastor asked me to pray for him. As I prayed he was touch by the Lord, brought into the presence of the Most High King. This was like no other service I had ever been to. Forty-one people were slain in the spirit. The pastor went down twice, then again when I tried to hug him bye. He was so drunk with the wine of the spirit, they had to carry him home. God's power had expressed itself in such a way that no one could deny it was God. I was touched in a new realm and lifted up into the glory of his presence one more time.

The next few months went by quickly. I had a different speaking engagement almost every other weekend. The word about my healing was sweeping all over the country.

The Albany church wanted me to be a guest at the women's camp they were having in March. They asked me to speak at the sunrise service. I quickly accepted and looked forward to what was to come. The theme of the meeting was *Wine and Dine in '99*. I knew we were going to sit at the feet of our Lord and worship him with our whole hearts. We took communion every day. It was great. We had the sunrise service in the rose garden. It was beautiful. About twenty women got up very early just to come. They were as blessed as I was. Our Lord never ceases to amaze me. He is so worthy of our praise.

Chapter 26

BOBBY HEALED IN MY LIVING ROOM

Spring was in the air and my days were going great. One morning in March, 1999 I had a phone call. This woman on the other end of the line acted so excited when I answered the phone. She asked, "Are you Donna Lee, the one who prays for people?"

I said, "yes."

She said, "My husband needs a twenty-two thousand dollar surgery and we need eleven thousand dollars up front within the week. He is in so much pain."

As I listened to the desperation in her voice, I knew I had to believe for her husband's healing. Our God is no respecter of persons. I knew he healed me and he would also heal him. I told her to call me in the morning and we would set up a time to meet. Before I had even hung up the phone, the Lord had confirmed in my spirit that I was to pray for her husband. They were from Comanche, Texas. Her husband had been out of work and he couldn't move his neck or shoulders. His name was Bobby Davis.

The next morning we scheduled them to come to our house in two days. It just happened to be the day he was supposed to have his surgery. From the point when said I would pray for them, everything you could ever imagine went wrong. My children were fighting. The Mazda quit running. The motor in my husband's car burned up. My son had gone swimming and burst his eardrum. And most of this happened the day they were going to arrive at 6:00 p.m. I had been fighting Satan all day, and I really wasn't in the mood for company. As I went into the bathroom to try to pull myself together, my husband called out my name and said, "Honey, they're here."

I went to the door and introduced myself. I had not seen any of these people before. It was a man and three ladies. They introduced themselves as Bobby, Michelle, his mom, and a friend. When Bobby came in, he started looking around, and then he saw the pictures on my wall and started smiling from ear to ear. He told me a little about himself. He was injured at work and was in so much pain, that when he would try to lift his arm up he would almost cry. He said, "I have never felt pain like that before."

I asked him if he believed the Word of God and that the Lord went to the cross for our sins, and if he was saved, did he know being saved is the greatest miracle of all. I said, "Do you know that our Lord took the stripes on his back for our healing, not just mine but yours also? It was done 2000 years ago; we just have to find it in the Word; stand on it, and wait for it to come to pass."

He said, "I know that our Lord heals today and I know that tonight is my night and the Lord is going to heal me."

I was so impressed by their awesome faith. There was no doubt at all in the room. We have such and awesome God. I shared my testimony with them as we all sat in the living room with tears running down our cheeks. His wife, Michele told me that they had prayed, "Lord if it is your will for this woman to pray for us, let us find her in two phone calls."

Her mom had heard me speak at the women's *Wine and Dine* meeting at the sunrise service. She didn't know my name or how to find me, but as she and Bobby prayed, my face flashed before their eyes, and they knew I was to pray for Bobby. On their second phone call, I picked up the phone. Now they were here and waiting for the Lord to come through. The expectation was high. Our faith reached into the heavenly realm and waited on the Lord's Word to come to pass. As we gathered around Bobby and started praying, there was such heaviness all around

I rebuked it and went on thanking God for total healing from the top of his head, to the tips of his toes.

Then the Lord said, *Lift his arms up.* I knew that Bobby had told me he couldn't lift his arms because the pain was so bad he would fall to his knees. Then I heard the Lord in my spirit said again, *Lift his arms and he will be healed.*

Without hesitation I said, "Yes Lord," and I lifted his arms and he fell to the ground. The heaviness that we had felt immediately left the room. He lay there for the longest time just smiling. You could see the glory on his face. When he got up, he was totally healed. He was raising his arms moving his neck and dancing around my living room. Everyone was so excited The Lord had not only used me, but Jimmy and everyone in the room to pray and believe for healing. Just to be able to experience the glory on his face was worth it all.

Then before he left he told me that the Lord had showed him my living room in a dream before he was ever sick. He saw people around him in a circle praying. He said, "This was your living room. Now I know what the Lord was telling me. Wow, we have a great God."

A few weeks went by and I received a phone call. Michele was pregnant. Then she told me they couldn't have children. The Lord had totally healed Bobby. I didn't even realize they were trying to have a baby. Now the Lord had sent them another blessing, the baby they always dreamed of but knew, without a miracle it would never come to pass. Now the miracle had come, total healing from the top of his head to the tips of his toes. Bobby has now begun his ministry; he is the pastor of a cowboy church.

Chapter 27

COMANCHE CHURCH

The months following went by quickly. I had many other churches calling me to come and speak. The miracles were many. The pastor from Comanche heard about Bobby's healing and asked me to come and share.

This time was so different. It was at the United Pentecostal Church. I told my testimony and ministered the Word of God. When I walked in, there was a different spirit there. I felt it one other time when I was in the hospital. As I was sharing I kept hearing this voice say, *Who are you to be speaking? You are not a preacher or evangelist. Did your God really do that?* I tried not to listen to it. I just continued to tell what our glorious God had done for me. When I had finished my testimony I asked for the pastor to come up so we could see if anyone needed prayer. I called for people to come forth who wanted prayer. As the people lined up for prayer, I assured them that it had nothing to do with me and the Lord was on the scene. Then I heard this voice once more. *Who are you to be praying for the sick? You are not a preacher or evangelist. Are you sure the Lord called you to do this? Are you equipped to pray for the sick and see them healed? You are nobody. Do you think your God will hear your prayers?* I looked over at the pastor standing beside me to see if she heard the voice that I was hearing. I knew immediately that I was hearing Satan himself trying to discourage me. He thought he could make me doubt what our Lord had done so far and what he was going to do.

I stopped the service and boldly said, "Satan you are a liar and I plead the blood of Jesus. The Lord called me and appointed me himself, to do his work." The Word says greater works will I do than even he did when he walked on this earth.

Verily, verily, I say unto you, He that believeth on me, the works that I do shall he do also; and greater works than these shall he do; because I go unto my Father (John 14:12 KJV).

The Spirit of the Lord GOD is upon me; because the LORD hath anointed me to preach good tidings unto the meek; he hath sent me to bind up the brokenhearted, to proclaim liberty to the captives, and the opening of the prison to them that are bound; To proclaim the acceptable year of the LORD, and the day of vengeance of our God; to comfort all that mourn (Isa. 61:1-2 KJV).

Then all the sudden the voice got smaller and smaller. I stopped and said, "Lord if this is not what you want me to be doing and if you are not in this I don't want any part of it." Then peace entered the room and I knew in my spirit I was in the right place.

Next in line was this woman. She had a glow around her from the top of her head all the way to the floor. She came up and just smiled at me. Her eyes were like a crystal blue ocean. When she approached me, I felt the anointing so strong. It was like the Lord had filled me up with his power and glory. I felt as though I had received a double portion of love. She just stood there looking deep into my eyes and smiling. I just kept praising God. Then she turned and walked away.

After I finished praying for everyone in the line, a woman called me over to her. I knew as soon as I approached her she had a demon spirit. I had fought those demons in the hospital and I recognized the spirit as one not from God. She told me she was possessed by demons and she wanted them out. At first I didn't know what to say, but I knew our Lord had given us power over Satan. I did all I knew to do. I told them to leave in Jesus' name. This woman started coughing and coughing. I just kept pleading the blood and telling them to get out in Jesus' name. I reminded them of their future and told them they had to leave. Finally, she stopped coughing and they were all gone. She looked like a totally different person. This was the first time I had ever cast the devil out of anyone, and I hoped it would be the last.

I quickly hugged her bye and started looking for that other woman. The one that was so anointed. I asked my husband where she had gone and I described her to him. He said, "Donna there was no women like that."

I said, "Oh yes there was. I saw her." But he assured me that there was no woman like that. I was puzzled.

We said bye to everyone and left for home. We arrived home and it was already dark. The next morning the pastor called to talk to me. I asked him who the woman was that had the golden glow around her and I told him how she looked and what she was wearing. He told me there was no such woman. "We have no one that goes to our church that looks like that." Then the pastor said, "The Lord must have sent you an angel to let you know you were right were he wanted you, doing what he had called you to."

That night when I went to sleep I was praying if it could be true. Could the Lord send me an angel to rescue me from that demon spirit. As I went to sleep and began to dream, she came to me just smiling. Our Lord God had sent me a sign. Oh, how I love him. The next morning I called everyone and told them about the angel. Nothing surprises me about our God. He is so wonderful.

Chapter 28

WOMEN'S MEETINGS

Over the next few months, the Lord kept opening doors for me. It had been one year and eight months since my healing and every day was a new adventure. The Lord opened a door for a women's meeting in Abilene at the Ramada Inn and even sent us a pastor to sponsor it. We met a lot of really special people and even had three speakers from different churches, Reitha Bryan, Joanne Jackson and Lala Scott. It was a pleasure and a joy to minister with these women. The Lord taught me so much through them. The denominational walls were coming down. We were just women and men who loved Jesus.

He gave me the name for my ministry as I prayed one day – Healing Heart Ministries, but our meetings were called The Women of the Word.

We would have our women's meeting on Saturday. People would come off the freeway and come into the motel to see what we were doing. Several told us that they were led there by the Lord not knowing why, but they would stay to listen and were always blessed. Soon they started coming and bringing friends to our monthly meeting. We always had a time of prayer and an invitation for people to be saved.

Being saved is the greatest miracle and gift from God, greater than any healing that we can ever receive. The Lord gave his only son.

Many people got healed and received Jesus at our meetings. I shared my testimony, and Reitha, Lala, and Joanne taught from the Bible. We all helped with worship and praise. We would have about seventy-five people in attendance at every meeting. Pastor Randy would set up the equipment for our music and help where he was needed. A lot of people from different churches helped set up tables and make refreshments. We are so blessed. The power of God was so apparent.

I spoke at Pastor Randy's church and he wanted to put me on prime time Christian TV. He wanted me to share my testimony with the world and he would set it up for me to go on the Janet Pollard Show. He believed in my testimony, so he paid for it. I was so excited, now I could share with millions of people through TV. As I shared my testimony, lots of people called to receive Jesus and were prayed for. Even to this day I still get cards and letters from people that were touched.

My sister called me one day when I was getting ready to go to our meeting. She asked me to pray for her assistant manager's brother. He had AIDS and was in the hospital weighing only seventy pounds. She knew the Lord had healed me and wanted me to pray for him. I sent him a prayer cloth and called his mom at the hospital. She was in his room. I asked her if he was saved and if he believed that our Lord could heal him. She asked him while I was on the phone and he said, "Yes, our Lord does heal. That's why he took the stripes on his back for our healing, and I have accepted him as my Savior. So I know if I was to die today I would be with him in heaven. The Word says to be absent from the body is to be with the Lord."

Then his mom told me the doctors had given up all hope. At the rate he was losing weight, he was going to die soon. But our Lord likes to show up when there is nothing else the doctors can do. He uses doctors but sometimes we need the Great Physician. When they think it's medically impossible, it's always possible with our God. We prayed and believed for his healing. Weeks went by and my sister called me to tell me that he was out of the hospital and he had started gaining weight immediately. The doctor's couldn't find any AIDS in his body. The Lord had come through and healed him. Praise God! Now he was sharing what the Lord had done for him with everyone.

I am now on only two pills a day and off all of my heart medicine. As I finish this book it has been six years. The doctor turned off my defibrillator and ran a stress test on my heart with it never missing a beat. I told him he could just leave it off, I didn't need it but he still turned it back on. The doctors are still amazed by the healing the Lord performed. The doctor released me and told me I was doing so well that I didn't have to make any future appointments to see him.

I pray that this book touches your heart and you realize that our Lord is the same yesterday, today, and forever. He is no respecter of persons. The healing and life I received, you can have also. All you have to do is ask and believe in your heart that Jesus died on a cross for your sins. He arose in three days for you and for me. The Bible says if you ask he will come in and live with you, and you too can know the love of Christ, which passeth knowledge, that you might be filled with all the fullness of God's Glory and grace.

Then you will truly know in your heart that what is said in the Word of God is what you and I need for our everyday life. Once you get a hold of the truth you will know that he is the only true answer.

I will not cease to give thanks for all that our Lord has done for me and what God our Lord Jesus Christ, the Father of glory, may give unto you—the spirit of wisdom and revelation in the knowledge of him. I pray the eyes of your understanding be enlightened and you may know the hope of his calling, the riches of the glory for your life and the exceeding greatness of his power to us that believe.

May God Bless You.

If you accepted Christ today please write me and let me know so I can join the angels in heaven as they dance around the throne. The Word says that they have a party for each soul saved.

Healing Heart Ministries
Donna Lee
lee_d2@hotmail.com

To order additional copies of

Have your credit card ready and call:

1-877-421-READ (7323)

or please visit our web site at
www.pleasantword.com

Also available at:
www.amazon.com
and
www.barnesandnoble.com

Printed in the United States
35200LVS00007B/100-156